COMPILATION OF RESEARCH - A HANDBOOK (EDITION 3)

LAW ESSENTIALS JOURNAL

Contents

CHAPTER ONE

THE IPS METHOD POSITIVELY PROTECT JUDICIAL DATA ON E-COURT APPLICATION IN SUPREME COURT INDONESIA

Syarifah Farrah Rizka Putri[1], Taswanda Taryo*[1], Agung Budi Susanto[1], Afzal Sayed Munna[2]

[1]*Graduate Studies of Magister for Informatics Engineering, University of Pamulang-UNPAM, Jalan Raya Puspiptek, Serpong 15310, Tangerang Selatan, Banten, Indonesia*

[2]*University of Sunderland in London, United Kingdom*

[2]*University of Wales Trinity Saint David, London, United Kingdom*

[2]*London Metropolitan University, United Kingdom*

[2]*UNICAF University, Ireland*

Abstract: In 2018, Supreme Court Indonesia, called Mahkamah Agung, carried out a major judicial reform by issuing a monumental policy which is a developed collaboration between the justice system and the development of information technology. The launch of the e-Court application is a breakthrough that has been developed and it is a public service application launched by the Supreme Court. The e-Court application is targeted at registered users and in the running e-Court application, a new security system is needed and functions to secure data in the e-Court database from data theft, user abuse and hacking. It takes a preventive measure to protect network security and information in an application or a program. Intrusion Prevention System (IPS) is a system that has a new approach to network defense systems. The IPS system is a collaboration between Intrusion Detection System (IDS) and the IP table. This system is able to detect if there is an intruder that will attack the local network, besides that the IPS system can also record all logs that are identified as entering e-Court network.By using a signature that functions as a traffic detector in the network, the preventive process is more optimal. Signatures matching and protocol parse are 2 stages in the IPS protocol detection procedure. Signature matching is where IPS abstracts the traffic protocol elements that allow for signature matches. The implementation of the IPS method, which has a variety of good working mechanisms, is able to make the e-Court application security system more secure in terms of data security. The mechanism of the IPS method has various types that have their respective advantages and greatly contribute as a form of prevention against forms of cybercrime especially in the country.

Keywords: *Supreme court of Indonesia, e-Court, IPS method, cybercrime*

INTRODUCTION

The world evolves over time and throughout history, the formation of countries in this world is clear, including the Sovereign State of the Republic of Indonesia. If we look at past history, we can see that the formation of the Indonesian state started from the thoughts of a group of young people. The state subsequently evolved into a well-formed organization and created a sovereign and independent state. And this also happened to the Supreme Court and it also made major changes. Judging from the history that happened, the establishment of the Unitary State of the Republic of Indonesia coincided with the birth of the Supreme Court. The Supreme Court began to exercise judicial power in 1945. Based on article 19, Law no. 19 of 1964, "The President can be directly involved in judicial matters. Until 1999, all judicial bodies were returned to the Supreme Court in accordance with Law no. 35 of 1999 which is known as the "one roof system". The one-roof trial is in accordance with the Article 11, which is understood as the result of legal reform and post-1998 judicial reform [1].

In 2018, the Supreme Court carried out a major judicial reform and by issuing a monumental policy which is a collaboration between the justice system and the development of information technology. This policy contained Supreme Court Regulation No. 3 of 2018 concerning Electronic Court (e-Court) Case Administration [2]. This foundation is also reinforced by public opinion that feels that conventional courts do not have the value of transparency, high in cost, take a long time and are complicated, causing the Constitutional Court to launch an e-Court application that can be a solution to all problems taking place. The e-Court application is a public service application launched by Supreme Court Indonesia. The e-Court application is targeted at registered users. The e-Court application includes several parts, including an online judicial registration application (e-filling), an online court fee payment application (e-payment), an online summons application (e-summons) and an online court application (e-litigation) [3]. The e-Court application, aside from making it easier from a judicial perspective, has several problems. From the point of view of the system, the problem of missing data and the security of data stored in the internal system.

Throughout 2020, there have been many cases of data theft and many cases of data leaks are reported to have occurred between May and November 2020. In this data leakage case, the data theft carried out is the personal data of an application accessor and is sold to dark forums [4]. The stolen data is the personal data of those who access an application. Therefore, it is needed an information security system that can solve the existing problems. Besides that, as an anticipatory step so that similar incidents do not occur in the future. In addition to the problem of data theft, similarities in terms of data, data records that are not stored properly are also problems that occur in the current e-Court system [5]. Data security is a set of processes and practices in terms of protecting the information technology that is important to people involved [6]. Viewed today, there are many information technology crimes and of all types of data security, authentication and encryption is one part of the current type of data security [6] and the Intrusion Prevention System (IPS) method can be the right choice. The IPS method is a network security technology or prevention where this method checks the flow of network traffic. The method is also useful for detecting and preventing exploitation of vulnerabilities [7]. It is hoped that the implementation of the IPS method can be a preventive measure as well as a solution. The IPS method, which emphasizes prevention, is considered quite good as a solution in the rise of data theft. By actively analyzing and quickly taking automatic action on all data traffic flows that enter the network is one of the characteristics of the IPS method, so that this factor makes prevention easier to do [8].

LITERATURE REVIEW

E-Court

According to expert opinion, the judiciary and the court have different meanings. Quoted from the opinion of R. Subekti and R. Tjitrosoedibio, "The court (rechtbank, court) is a body that is a subject in conducting trials, where the task is to examine and decide on legal disputes and violations of laws. And still in the opinion of R Subekti and R Tjitrosoedibio, "judicial (rechtspraak, judiciary) is all things that are related and have something to do with the duty of a state in upholding law and justice [9]. In this case, the justice system in developing countries has undergone a revolution and change which has begun to combine with currently developing technology. One of the breakthroughs that are currently being started is e-Court application. E-Court applications have developed in many other countries and one of them is Indonesia. E-Court itself was firstly developed by the Republic of Korean (RoK) and started from the judiciary in collaboration with the Korean Institute of Science and Technology in 1979. In 1986, the computerization of the first civil court in the Korea began and the RoK itself has had a network of more than 28 courts since 1995 [10]. E-Court itself was born from a problem faced in the judiciary today. Based on the Indonesia Ombudsman report, almost 394 complaints were recorded between 2014-2016 regarding extortion that occurred in the judicial process, namely, 215 reports about pending cases and 117 reports about the incompetence of the Supreme Court in carrying out performance in the judicial system [11]. The judiciary which is considered no longer transparent, has a high cost and justice which is considered by society to be only the owner of a few people in power, makes a judicial revolution that collaborates with technology becomes the best solution.

The e-Court application itself consists of several integrated functions and based on sources quoted from the website of the Supreme Court, e-Courts have the meaning of a service for registered users. In e-Courts, there are various services that can be used by the public, among others [12], namely, a) e-Filing (Online Case Registration in Court), b) e-Payment (Online Case Fee Payment) and c) e-Summons (Online Party Summons). E-Courts themselves already have a legal umbrella as stated in the Regulation of Supreme Court Indonesia No. 3, 2018 concerning Case Administration.

Network Security

According to (Iwan Sofana, 2008), computer networks are a set of inter-connections of a number of autonomous computers. With the occurrence of a computer network or computer networks, there is an exchange of information. When there is an exchange of information, a system is needed to maintain the security of the information. There are 2 security that must be created in a computer network, namely, information security and network security itself. According to (Rahardjo, 2002), information security is how we can prevent fraud or detect fraud in an information-based system, where the information itself has no physical meaning. Meanwhile, according to (Binanto, 2007), network security is a system of protection against the network and its applications from attacks or activities that could threaten the validity and integrity of data [13].

Network Security has several basic principles such as, a) Confidentiality, where objects contained in a network may not be shared with other users who do not have access rights, b) Integrity which means that each object received must have originality, which requires authenticity of information from the source to the user and c) Availability means that each user has access to objects or information. There are various types of threats in network security, including, one, probe, also known as probing, is an attempt to access the system in order to obtain information about the system. Two, account compromise is the illegal use of a computer account by someone who is not the owner of the account. Three, Root Compromise is abuse of account privileges, where the impact is system performance can change. Four, Packet Sniffer is a program that can capture data from packets passing through the network. Five, Denial of Service (DoS) aims to prevent users from getting services from the system. Where an attacker can flood the network with a large amount of power, resulting in a pending network connection. Six, IP Spoofing is an attack model, where the attack changes a person's device so that it bypasses firewall protection. Seven, DNS Forgery is a way for someone to steal important data from other users, so that the data can be misused [14]. Responding to the current problem of security breaches, where systems such as firewalls have not been able to anticipate attacks from within the network and cannot do much to explain attack behavior or anomalies. Anti-virus software also has the limitation of recognizing new virus patterns before any antivirus program is created. Intrusion Detection also only sends a warning after an attack enters the network and has no power to stop security attacks.

Intrusion Prevention System (IPS)

It takes a preventive measure to protect network security and information in an application or program. Intrusion Prevention System (IPS) is a system that has a new approach to network defense systems. Where IPS combines firewall techniques with Intrusion Detection better, by using more proactive techniques. Where IPS prevents attacks to enter the network by examining various data records and using sensors that detect patterns. So that when the attack is identified, the system automatically performs intrusion prevention and logs deviant data [15]. IPS is used to provide warnings against attacks in the network as well as provide preventive measures with the Firewall function mechanism (data link layer, network layer, transport layer and application layer) and IDS. This task can be an innovation in the future, where IPS functions as a gateway, perimeter defense, all-in-all capability and network prevention inspection [16].

According to [17] Schonlau et al., 2001 it takes a different environment in order to study the effects of certain changes. Which is common practice to keep all other variables constant. The explanation from [18] can use social cognitive theory and explore existing behavior in order to understand what factors influence user behavior. In addition, based on the results of research [18], the automatic grouping into certain clusters can show that the mechanism is effective for detecting attacks. Based on [19], presenting a social cognitive theory explaining the interaction between behavioral, personal and environmental factors can be analyzed through a questionnaire.

Based on data obtained from [19], Indonesia experiences cyber attacks every day as many as 1.225 billion where the data is strengthened by the Coordinating Ministry for Politics, Law and Security. This has happened since 2018 until now. According to the Head of the Information and Communication Technology Infrastructure Development Division of the East Java Communications and Information Service, Djoko Purwono, quoted from [20], starting from 2012, 50% of government websites have been hacked. And the other 50% are websites with public domains. The most obvious reason why many government websites are under attack. One of them is someone's dissatisfaction with the services or data displayed on the website or application. Based on the data [21], the danger that is no less serious is the crime of the application user itself. What we need to know, computer network security is supported by 2 factors, namely internal and external factors. Where currently the security of internal factors is a challenge that must be solved in the future.

RESEARCH METHOD

Research Activities

Based on Figure 1, the research flow can be explained as follows, a) problem formulation and it is needed to clearly formulate a problem in order to find the right solution; b) goal setting process is required and hence the process of setting goals for the system can be built; c) Literature Study and this step is needed to look for sources that will be used as the right reference; d) Data collection and this process is mandatory to collect data as a support for making the system; e) Topology Design which is required to develop the design process of a network topology that will be implemented in the system; f) input and output and those are all forms of input from outside and from within as a support in making the system; g) System Design is dedicated to design an appropriate system according to needs, based on the problems explored; h) System Configuration needed to focus on configuring the system to be as expected; i) Implementation which is the application of the system that has been created and j) Testing which is a trial process in running the system in order to see the overall final result.

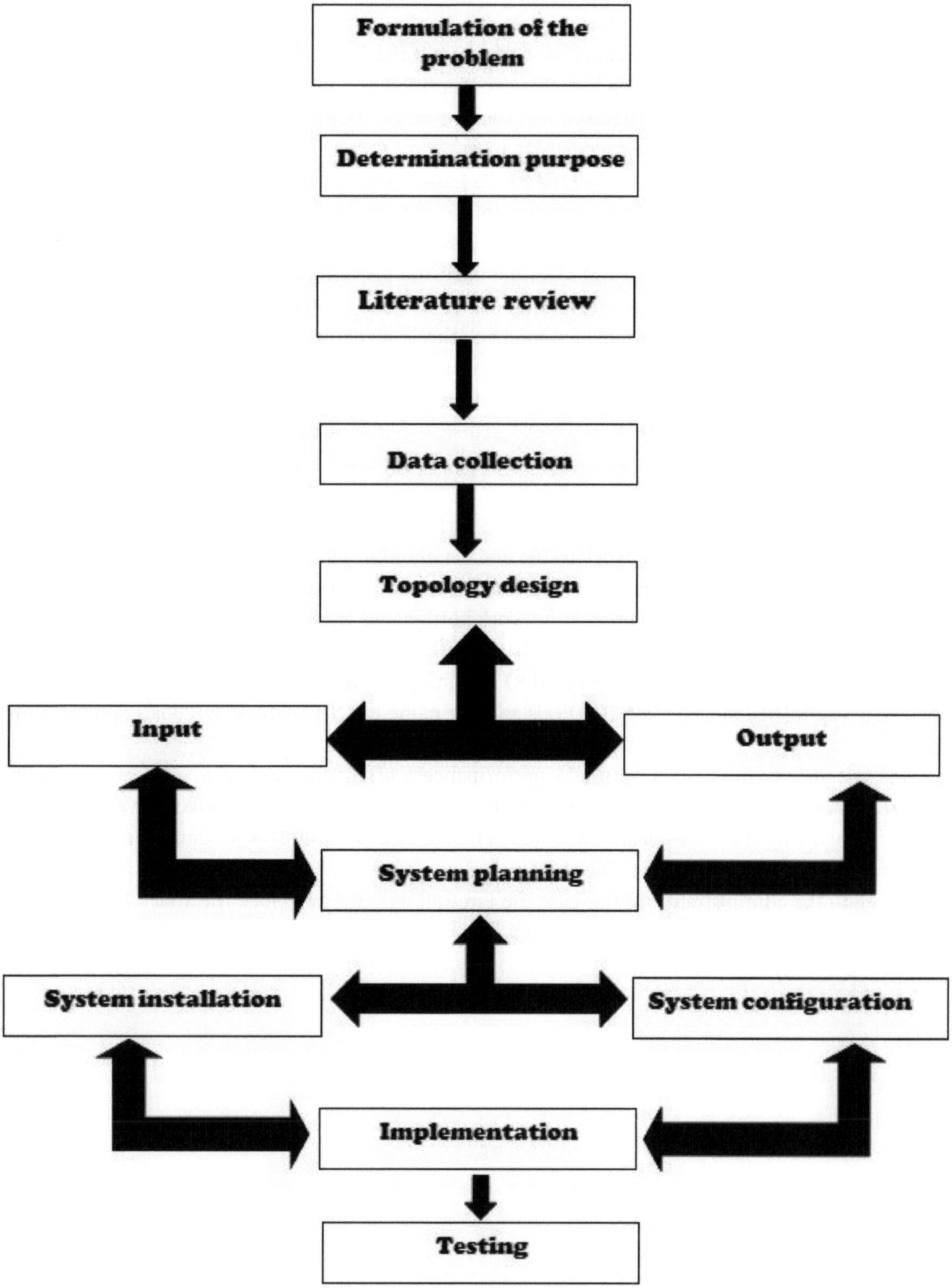

Figure 1. Flow Chart of Research Activities.

Intrusion Prevention System (IPS) Intrusion Prevention System is a good security system that can detect all activities that are considered suspicious for the system. This system emphasizes more on the form of preventive action. The protected data will then be more protected with this system. The IPS system is a collaboration between the IDS system and the IP table. This system is able to detect if there is an intruder that will attack the local network, besides that the IPS system can record all logs that are identified as entering our network. By using a signature that functions as a traffic detector in the network, then the preventive or preventive process is more optimal. Intrusion Prevention System consists of the following expalanation.

Host-based Intrusion Prevention System (HIPS) [22] and HIPS is a prevention system that consists of multiple layers of security. HIPS has several characteristics in the system, including, Packet Filtering which is a security technology that functions to regulate packets that are given access to enter the system or network in accordance with established rules. Status inspection and real time intrusion prevention keep the host in an efficient and feasible state. HIPS has a working mechanism by preventing malicious code from trying to enter the host, where the code is expected not to be executed and is not needed to check threat signatures. With the direct installation of the HIPS agent program, the resulting system is protected and the activities of its internal systems can be monitored. Kernel system and operating system services are systems that are often bound with HIPS. This is intended so that HIPS can monitor and block system calls that are considered suspicious for the purpose of preventing intrusions to the host. Besides that, HIPS also has other advantages, namely being able to monitor the flow of data and activities in a particular application.

Network-based Intrusion Prevention System (NIPS) which is in-line proactive protection has the advantage of being able to withstand all forms of network traffic and can monitor all forms of activity and suspicious codes. High performance is one of the crucial elements in IPS devices and this is due to the use of in-line models. However, the use of the in-line model is intended to prevent network bottlenecks from occurring. So, when designing NIPS, three components are needed which aim to accelerate bandwidth performance. In addition to monitoring one host, the Network-based Intrusion Prevention System (NIPS) also inspects and secures one network globally. In-Line IDS or also called Gateway Intrusion Detection (GIDS) is another name for NIPS where, NIPS is a combination of IPS with firewall.

IPS work system has similarities with IDS performance and IDS has a way to protect computer systems by detecting attacks and then stopping them. In the initial processing, IDS tends to take preventive action against an intrusion by recognizing the cause of the intrusion. The method used by IDS in identifying it is by comparing an event that is considered suspicious with the signs stored on the system. When an intrusion is readable, the IDS will issue a warning to the administrator. In this case the Firewall will directly block the attack which is suspected as an intrusion [22].

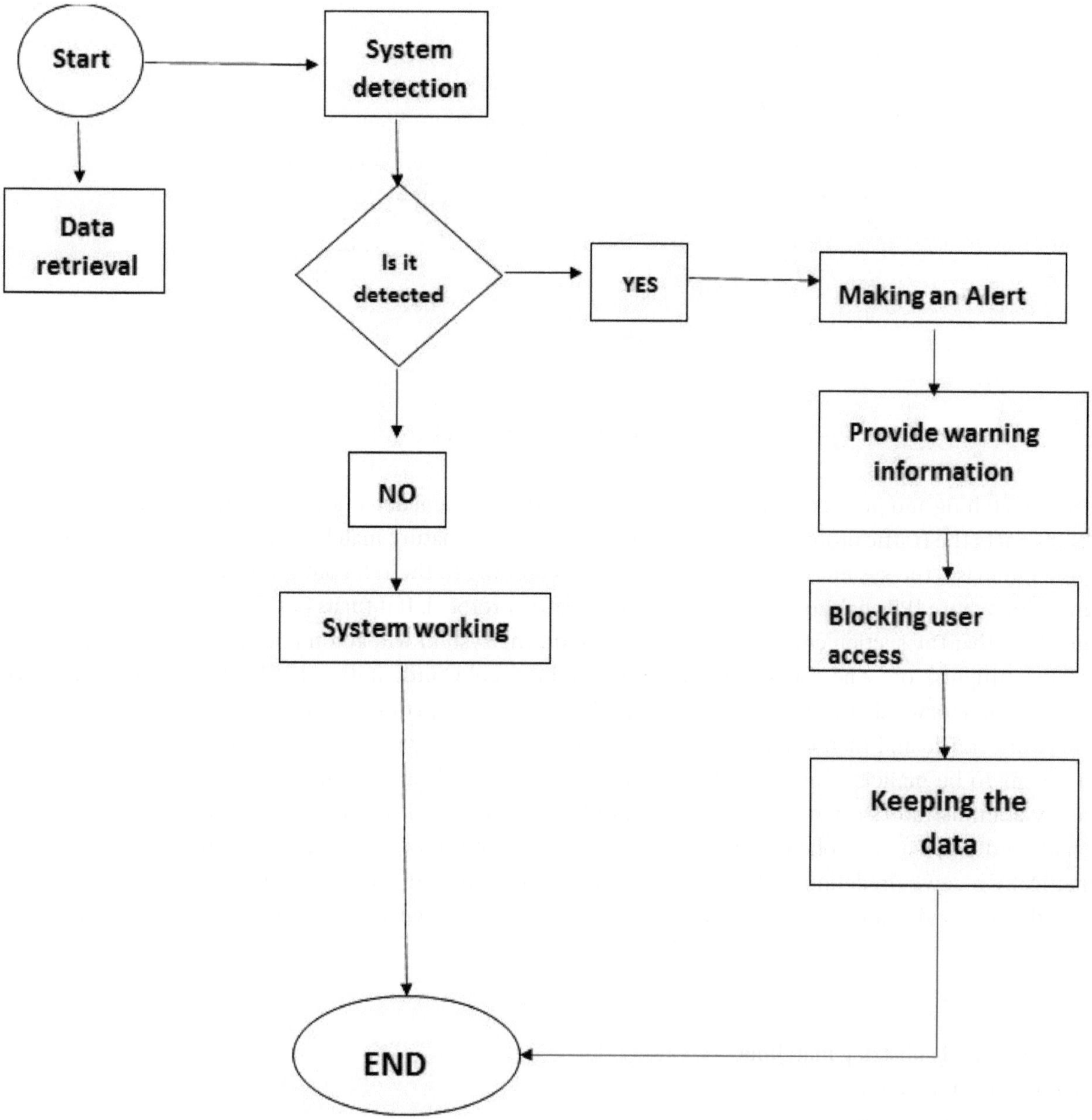

Figure 2. Method of Instrusion Prevention System (IPS).

RESULTS AND DISCUSSIONS

Intrusion Prevention System is a network security device that functions to monitor and respond to potential threats. IPS can determine possible threats by examining network traffic. A prevention system that manages automatic responses to threats, based on rules set by network administrators. IPS has several main functions, including identifying suspicious activities, recording relevant information, blocking these activities and reporting them. IPS can be used for other purposes, including identifying problems with security policies, documenting threats, and preventing individual policy violations. IPS besides being included in the firewall, IPS is also anti-virus software, and anti-spoofing software.

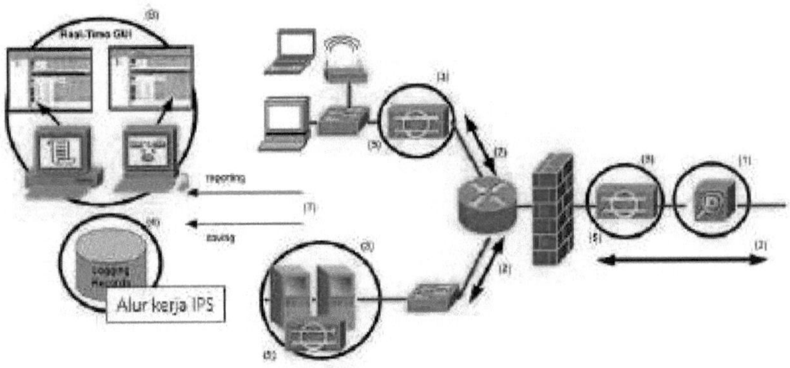

Figure 3. Network Security Device of IPS.

Signatures matching and protocol parse are 2 stages in the IPS protocol detection procedure. Signature matching is where IPS abstracts the traffic protocol elements that might have a signature match. If there are matching elements in the signature database, the system will process the traffic according to the IPS configuration action. While Protocol Parse is an action where IPS analyzes part of the network traffic protocol. If it turns out that the results of the analysis carried out show that the section contains abnormal content, the system will automatically process the traffic based on the action configuration. And this section is called the Protocol Configuration [26]. IPS actively scans network traffic, which is then forwarded as malicious activity and detects attack patterns based on stored data. The IPS system analyzes network traffic and then compares the bitstream with a stored or known internal database. IPS may block packets it deems to be malicious and then take action by blocking all future traffic to the attacker's IP address or port. Security administrators can define IPS policies to be applied to IPS machines. The IPS engine can be applied to the default and custom IPS policies according to the administrator's requirements to apply to access rules. IPS can automatically receive predefined intrusion prevention and security updates. The IPS can also perform complex analyses, such as observing and reacting to suspicious patterns. These mechanics include [23] the followings:

1. Address matching
2. HTTP string and substring matching
3. General pattern matching
4. Analyze TCP connection
5. Packet anomaly detection
6. Traffic anomaly detection
7. TCP/UDP port matching The Intrusion Prevention System will record information regarding the event that occurred then notify the security administrator and provide a report. To help secure the network, IPS can automatically receive prevention and security updates to continuously monitor and block emerging Internet threats.

To deal with Intrusion Prevention System Countermeasures, IPS uses several response techniques that involve:

1. Change the security environment
– for example, by configuring a firewall to increase protection against previously unknown vulnerabilities.
2. Change the attack content
– for example, by replacing harmful parts of emails, such as fake links, with warnings about removed content.
3. Send automatic alarms to system administrators, notifying them of possible security breaches.
4. Take down malicious packages
5. Reset the connection.
6. Block traffic from offending IP addresses.

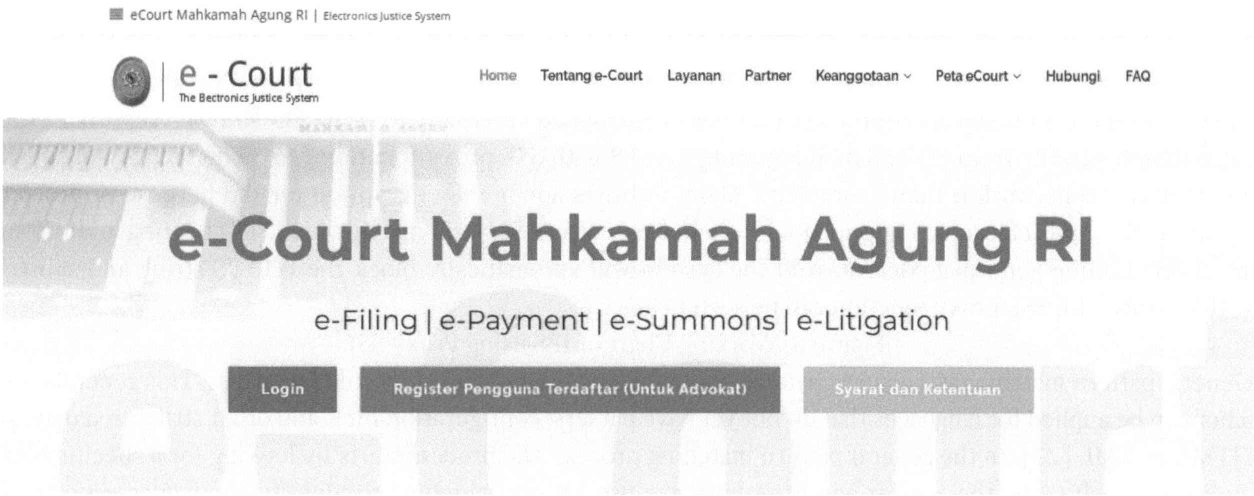

Figure 4. Website Display of Indonesia Supreme e-Court.

IPS signatures are categorized by protocol and can be identified by the signature ID. ID signatures have 2 parts: the protocol ID which consists of the first bit or the first and second bits, and the attacker ID. To get the best results in a security system, address matching is one of the IPS mechanisms in action or reaction to codes that harm the system. The address scanning system requires a supporting application that can scan IP addresses. Where this application is juxtaposed with the Intrusion Prevention System so that it can synergize properly. The system is carried out by conducting more than one inspection. And save data from ip address into 2 databases. One is the whitelist and blacklist [24].

Whitelist is a configuration option to allow security scanners to be used against a protected environment without being blacklisted. Intrusion Prevention System or IPS can block IP addresses that have attacked. Therefore, it is needed a supporting application that can scan IP addresses and Whitelist working system in scanning IP Address can be seen below.

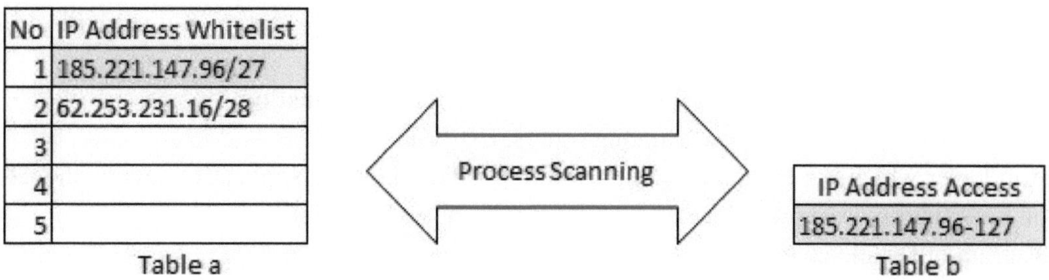

Figure 5. Whitelist Working System of IPS

The white list work system will start when the user accesses the web. When the user tries to access the web, supporting applications will scan the user's IP address. The applications will perform the configuration based on the stored database. Where IPS will block IP addresses that are not included in the whitelist but are on the blacklist, namely, IP addresses that have a history of trying to attack the web. So, automatically IP addresses that are not included in the whitelist will be directly blocked and cannot access.

Hypertext Transfer Protocol Secure (HTTPS) is a combination of the Hypertext Transfer Protocol (HTTP) with the Secure Sockets Layer (SSL) protocol. SSL is also known as Transport Layer Security which is abbreviated as TLC and TLC is a secure authentication protocol that has been applied externally to browsers and web servers [25]. IPS can also monitor traffic from HTTPS by integrating the IPS with SSL proxy function [26]. The security of sensitive data sent over the network is then guaranteed. Many websites adopt SSL encryption for the purpose of protecting information. SSL and IPS can be integrated with each other, where SLL will match which HTTP string and subscript it detects containing abnormal content. And the system will automatically block the HTTPS string and substring. How IPS works with SSL proxy function can be seen below.

Figure 6. Working Chart of IPS using Proxy SSL.

Generic pattern matching is a generic pattern matching technique in unsupported languages. This general pattern matcher can be applied for languages that do not yet have parsers, configuration files, and other structured data, such as, HTML or XML [27]. In the general pattern matching process, the process starts by looking for a specific pattern in the value specified by the user or admin. Admin can use pattern matching to identify some guess information, including social security number, phone number, postal code, or other information that matches the pattern. Pattern matching works by reading a text string to match a predefined pattern using a pattern match expression which is also known as the Regular Expression [28]. In the IPS method, pattern matching can be a good detection mechanism in which pattern matching can be a preventive mechanism for users who are detected as harmful to applications and data. The system will store user and guest data that has a pattern match as a malicious user or guest. Then, an automatically preventive action can be taken. Admins can create regular expressions that match the content in the data transmission. A transmission containing a string that matches the pattern in its data, so when there is a match, the IPS system will work [29].

Figure 7. Flowchart of Generic Pattern Recognition.

Transmission Control Protocol/Internet protocol (TCP) is a set of communication security protocols used as a liaison between hosts on the internet. TCP/IP uses two main protocols, namely, TCP and IP. TCP/IP was developed into the UNIX operating system and is used on the internet, thus becoming a standard for transmitting data over the network. TCP is also able to create two hosts to establish a connection and exchange data streams. TCP guarantees that the data sent will be in a systematic order as sent by the sender [30] and TCP has several layers, such as the followings:

1. Physical Layer that is determined by the characteristics of the transmission medium, signal coding scheme, system means of sending data to devices connected to the network
2. Data link layer which has a relationship with a logical - interface on one system and network, and is capable of fragmentation or defragmentation
3. Network layer that is concerned with routing data from source to destination
4. Transport layer which is divided into 2, among others, UDP and TCP
5. Application Layer which is a combination of session, presentation and application layers on OSI that provides communication between processes or applications on different hosts [31].

Figure 8. Diagram of Data Exchange between Client and Server.

The large number of network packets that are channeled into modern networks together with high transmission speeds can hinder the implementation of information technology security. Besides, the virtual network also creates a dynamic and flexible environment [32]. In network security, the anomaly detection system works together with the firewall and IPS is a very good collaboration. In the field of anomaly network detection, there are two different approaches, including flow-based, where this approach relies on network elements that function to create a flow of information for analysis. The second approach is packed based which directly analyzes data packet information to detect anomalies [33].

CONCLUSION AND FUTURE WORK

Conclusion

Based on the results of the analysis of the research on the implementation of the IPS method to protect judicial data in the e-Court application of Supreme Court Indonesia, several conclusions were obtained. One, the security of the application itself is now quite good. The Constitutional Court has done very well in maintaining the security of the data of those who access the application. Two, the implementation of the IPS method, which has a variety of good working mechanisms, is able to make the e-Court application security system more secure in terms of data security. Three, the mechanism of the IPS method has various types that have their respective advantages and greatly contribute as a form of prevention against forms of cybercrime. Four, preventive actions performed by the IPS method can be customized according to the administrator's needs. Indeed, the success of the Supreme Court in making breakthroughs in the field of technology should be highly appreciated. The existing security system so far is considered sufficient to anticipate the existing cybercrime. By implementing the IPS method, it is really expected that existing security can be improved.

Future Work

It is undeniable that the success of the existing security system in the current e-Court system is considered sufficient to ward off cybercrime that occurs. But, the growing technology causes the technology for cybercrime which also develops rapidly. So, rather than that, future solutions are needed that can be applied as suggestions that should be considered. In this case, the security technology advice that is suggested is the use of double layer security. It is suggested the use of the OTP system and face recognition system for guests who have been registered as users. OTP system stands for One Time Password [34] that is a one-time use password that will be sent to the user when logging into the e-Court application. The password will be sent directly to the registered user number when signing up for the first time. Meanwhile, Face Recognition Technology (FCT) is a facial recognition technology that is currently under development and the FCT utilizes artificial intelligence (AI) to recognize faces that have been stored in a database [35].

REFERENCES

[1] Mahkamah Agung,(2017), " Mahkamah Agung dalam Dinamika Perubahan", Accessed from https://www.mahkamahagung.go.id/id/artikel/2847/mahkamah-agung-dalam-dinamika-perubahan on 18 September 2021

[2] Ecourt, Mahkamah Agung,(2018), "Perma 03_2018.pdf-e court Mahkamah Agung RI". Accessed from https://ecourt.mahkamahagung.go.id/perma_03_2018.pdf on 23 September 2021.

[3] Ecourt, Mahkamah Agung(2018)," pengertian e court".

[4] Stephanie, Conney &Wahyudin, Reza (2021)," 7 Kasus Kebocoran Data yang terjadi sepanjang 2021". Accessed from https://tekno.kompas.com/read/2021/01/01/14260027/7 -kasus-kebocoran-data-yang-terjadi-sepanjang- 2020?page=all on 23 September 2021

[5] D Damie (2021)," Problems with e-court data- NIFPF". Accessed form https://www.nipfp.org.in/media/medialibrary/2020/07/ WP_314 2020.pdf on 23 September 2021.

[6] Varonis(2021),"Data Security: Importance, Types, and Solution". Accessed form https://www.varonis.com/blog/data-security/ on 23 September 2021

[7] Paloatonetworks (2021)," What is an Instrusion Prevention System?". Accessed fromhttps://www.varonis.com/blog/data-security/ on 22 September 2021.

[8] Ririn A, Iskandar F Novi DN (2018), "Jurnal Informatika Vol 18 No. 1, " Implementasi Instrusion Detection Systems (IDS) & Intrusion Prevention System (IPS) Berbasis Snort Server untuk Keamanan Jaringan Lain". Accessed from https://jurnal.darmajaya.ac.id/index.php/JurnalInformat ika/article/view/1118/pdf on 23 September 2021.

[9] Hufron & Rubea Advocates(2021)," Sistem Peradilan Indonesia". Accessed from https://www.advocates.id/sistem-peradilan-indonesia/ on 7 Oktober 2021

[10]Eng.scourt(2021),"History". Accessed from https://eng.scourt.go.kr/eng/judiciary/eCourt/history.jsp on 7 Oktober 2021

[11] Ptun.yogyakarta(2021)," E- court dan Masa Depan Sistem Peradilan Modern di Indonesia". Accessed form https://ptun-yogyakarta.go.id/index.php/artikel/193-e- court-dan-masa-depan-sistem-peradilan-modern-di-

indonesia.html. on 7 Oktober 2021.

[12] djkn. Kemenkeu.(2021) " E- court Berperkra Di Pengadilan Secara Elektronik". Accessed from https://www.djkn.kemenkeu.go.id/kpknl-manado/baca-artikel/12840/E-court-Berperkara-Di-Pengadilan-Secara-Elektronik.html On 7 0ktober 2021.

[13] Yoga Widya Pradipta, Asmunin (2017) ,"Jurnal manajemen Informatika. Volume 7 Nomer 1 Tahun 2017, 21-2, Implementasi Intrusion Prevention System (IPS) Menggunakan Snort dan Ip Tables Berbasis Linux". Accessed from htttps://ejournal.unesa.ac.id on 7 Oktober 2021 .

[14]Irfan Kurniadi H, Irsan Taufik Ali (2018),"Jurnal FTEKNIK Volume 5 Edisi 1 Januari s/d Juni 2018, Kajian Penerapan Metode Intrusion Prevention System di Jaringan Internet dan Intranet Universitas Riau". ". Accessed from https:// jom.unri.ac.id on 7 Oktober 2021.

[15] T. Ghorbani, A.A., Lu, W(2009)," *Network Intrusion Detection and Prevention : Concepts and Technique, Springer,* 2009". Accessed from https://researchgate.net on 7 Oktober 2021 .

[16] G. Ollmann(2003), "*Intrusion Prevention Systems (IPS) destined to replace legacy routers," Network Security, vol. 11*, 2003, pp. 18-19. Accessed from https://researchgate.net on 7 Oktober 2021

[17] E.E. Schultz and E. Ray(2007), "Future of Intrusion Prevention," *Computer Fraud & Security*, 2007, pp. 11-13. Accessed from https://researchgate.net on 7 Oktober 2021

[18] H.S. Rhee, C. Kim, and Y.U. Ryu(2009), "Self- efficacy in information security: Its influence on end users' information security practice behavior," Journal Computer & Security, vol. 28, 2009, pp. 816-826. Accessed from https://researchgate.net on 7 Oktober 2021.

[19] Kominfo(2021)." Indonesia Diserang Hacker Miliaran Kali Tiap Hari ." Accessed from https://kominfo.go.id/content/detail/11956/indonesia-diserang-hacker-miliaran-kali-tiap-hari/0/sorotan_media.on 7 Oktober 2021.

[20]kominfo (2021). " 50% Situs Pemerintahan Diserang Hacker". Accessed from https://kominfo.go.id/content/detail/1493/50-persen-situs-pemerintah-diserang-hacker/0/berita on 7 Oktober 2021.

[21] D. Stiawan, A.H. Abdullah, and M.Y. Idris(2010), "*The Prevention Threat of Behavior-based Signature using Pitcher Flow Architecture*," International Journal of Computer Science & Network Security, vol. 10, 2010, pp. 289-294. Accessed from https://ijcaonline.org on 7 Oktober 2021.

[22] DoddySuprianto, (2021)"*Intrusion Prevention System*". Accessed from http://doditsuprianto.blogspot.com/p/keamanan- jaringan-dengan-pengertian-ips.html on 21 Oktober 2021

[23] Barracuda (2021) , "How An IPS Works,database for known attack patterns". Accessed from https://www.barracuda.com/glossary/intrusion-prevention-system. on 21 Oktober 2021.

[24] Appcheck-ng(2021), "Whitelisting Appcheck on Your Firewalls and IPS" . Accessed from https://appcheck-ng.com/get-help/documentation/whitelisting-appcheck-on-your-firewalls-and-ips/. on 21 Oktober 2021

[25] Healthit.gov (2021) " What does https web address mean". Accessed from https://www.healthit.gov/faq/what-does-https-web-address-meanon 21 Oktober 2021.

[26] Hillstonenet (2021), " SSL Proxy Accessed from https://docs.hillstonenet.com/en/Content/9_Security/SSLProxy.htm?Highlight=ssl%20proxy%20function. on 21 Oktober 2021.

[27] Semegrep.dev (2021)" Generic Patten Matching". Accessed from https://semgrep.dev/docs/experiments/generic-pattern-matching/. on 10 November 2021

[28] Laserfiche(2021)" Pattern Matching". Accessed from https://www.laserfiche.com/support/webhelp/quickfields/8.0/en-us/content/pattern%20matching.htmon 10 November 2021.

[29] Sc1.checkpoint (2021)," Protection Data By Pattern". Accessed from https://sc1.checkpoint.com/documents/R81/WebAdminGuides/EN/CP_R81_DataLossPrevention_AdminGuide/Topics-DLPG/Protecting-Data-by-Pattern.htmon 10 November 2021.

[30] Stanford.edu (2021)," Transmission Control Protocol". Accessed from https://cs.stanford.edu/people/eroberts/courses/soco/projects/1999 00/internet/tcp.htmlon 10 November 2021.

[31] DM Mydza (2011) "Analisa Dan Konfigurasi Network Intrusion Prevention System (NIPS) Pada Linux Ubuntu 10.04 LTS". Accessed from http://repository.uinsuska.ac.id/665/1/2011_2011171.pdfon 10 November

2021

[32] Daniel Spiekermann, Jorg Keller(2021) "Unsupervised packet-based anomaly detection in virtual networks Accessed from https://www.sciencedirect.com/science/article/pii/S1389128621001286. On 10 November 2021.

[33] Hyu Anh nguyen,Deokjai coy(2021, " Network Anomaly Detection: Flow –based and Packet –Based". Accessed from https://arxiv.org/ftp/arxiv/papers/1007/1007.1266. pdf. On 10 November 2021.

[34]Daniel Nugraha (2021) "OTP, Definisi dan Fungsinya dalam Sistem Transaksi". Accessed from https://www.paper.id/blog/finansial-umkm/sistem- transaksi-otp/ on 17 November 2021.

[35] Centerklik(2021)" Teknologi Face Recognition : Pengertian Dan Cara Kerjanya Accessed from https://www.centerklik.com/teknologi-face-recognition/. On 17 November 2021.

CHAPTER TWO

Essential for a Tort- Legal Damage

Disha Puri*
**Student, Symbiosis Law School, Noida*

INTRODUCTION

Numerous events have been made to define 'tort' but the legal world has not come across a single definition that gives justice to the true essence of tort. On the basis of origin, the word, 'tort' can be traced to the Latin word *tortus* meaning, 'twisted' or 'crooked'. In the most basic terms, tort can be described as a wrong, civil in nature, against which law provides remedy.

Explaining the basis of tort law- "In the great majority of tort actions coming before the courts, the plaintiff is seeking monetary compensation (damages) for the injury he has suffered and this fact strongly emphasises the function of tort in allocating or redistributing loss"[1] The primary aim of tort law is to deliver relief to the injured party in the form of damages, as well as, impose punishment on the wrongdoers to set an example for the society so as to deter others to commit such wrongs.

On the basis of its elements, tort can be described as an act or omission that gives rise to injury or harm to another and amounts to a civil wrong for which the courts impose liability[2]. Injury means interference with an individual's legal rights, whereas, harm refers to the negative consequences on the plaintiff. For example, if 'A' parks her car in front of B's house which obstructs him to move outside his gate, A is interfering with B's legal right of enjoying free passage in front of his house, thereby causing him harm. Conclusively, A has committed a tort against B.

The primary objective of tort law is to deliver relief to the aggrieved party in the form of damages, as well as, impose punishment on the wrongdoers to set an example for the society so as to deter others to commit such wrongs. Common torts include- battery, assault, infliction of emotional and physical distress, trespass to property and individual etc.

Every person is entitled to some basic rights, constitutional or statutory and she can enjoy it without any sort of intrusion. Examples of such basic rights are right to liberty, freedom, vote, etc. The smallest of any legal injury against these basic rights is liable to be compensated with adequate measures even if it did not cause any damage to the plaintiff.

This maxim also enshrines the meaning of another legal maxim of *Ubi Jus ibi Remedium* or "wherever there is a legal right, there is a remedy". Tort law is concerned with liability, rather than punishment. Liability in torts is primarily imposed with compensation or in some cases, injunction.

RESEARCH OBJECTIVES

1. To understand the significance of legal damage as an element of torts
2. To research about the types of damages with various illustrations

DAMAGE AS CONSTITUENT OF LAW OF TORTS

Law of torts has two essential elements-

(A). Act or Omission

(B). Legal damage

EXPLAINING ACT OR OMISSION-

A wrongful act or omission must be committed in order to claim damages in case of torts. This act or omission can either be morally wrong or legally wrong. A legally wrong act is one that violates the legal rights of an individual.

EXPLAINING LEGAL DAMAGE-

To understand the maxim of injuria sine damnum, learning about the concept of damages is crucial. Damage means a harm or loss suffered by a person as a result of some wrongful act or omission by another person[3]. The court has a duty of compensating this damage. The sum of money given by the court as compensation is called "damages". With the advent of urbanisation and technology, particularly with the use of motor vehicles, the instances of tort damages have been on the rise.

On the nature of harm suffered by the plaintiff, damage is of two types: (i) absolute and (ii) qualified.

1. ABSOLUTE RIGHTS - In case of damage of an absolute right, the law conjectures damage although there is no monetary loss.
2. QUALIFIED RIGHTS - Qualified rights include two well-known maxims- injuria sine damnum and damnum sine injuria. Damnum sine injuria is actionable only after proving a certain degree of damage caused.

Damnum Sine Injuria means damage without injury. The court does not provide any action against it. Injuria Sine Damnum is explained in detail as below-

In case of damage of an absolute right, the law conjectures damage although there is no monetary loss.

CASE LAWS TO ELABORATE THE CONCEPT OF ABSOLUTE RIGHTS

Ashby v. White (1703) 2 Lord Rayam 938

FACTS:

The plaintiff' voting right, which was his legal right, in a parliamentary election was infringed by the defendant.

HELD:

The defendant was held accountable even though there was no pecuniary loss to the plaintiff. This is because the absolute right (right to vote) of the plaintiff was surpassed. Justice Holt ruled: "Every injury imports a damage, though it does not cost the party one farthing, and it is impossible to prove the contrary for a damage is not merely pecuniary, but an injury imports a damage, when a man is thereby hindered of his right"[4]

While talking about qualified rights, there is no presumption of legal right and the interference of a qualified right is only actionable after the consequent damage or injury to the plaintiff is proven.

The following are the essential ingredients of the legal damage:

1. There must be interference with a legal right (absolute or qualified)
2. It must have resulted in a damage or injury in the eye of law
3. The damages caused should be proved in case it's a tort committed against an absolute right and not a qualified right

Qualified rights include two well-known maxims- *Injuria Sine Damno* and *Damnum Sine Injuria*. These are actionable only after proving a certain degree of damage caused. Both the maxims can be broken down into the following parts-

1. Damno/Damnum means harm or loss in respect to property, health, money, possessions etc
2. Injuria means an infringement to the legal rights an individual possesses
3. Sine means without

INJURIA SINE DAMNO

This maxim literally means legal injury without any damage or harm. There is a violation of the legal rights of an individual without any substantial harm or loss caused to them. The law guarantees all individuals the right to their property, liberty, life, immunity and the violation to these rights is *actionable per se*, i.e., to claim damages against the violation of these rights, harm or damage does not have to be proven. Moreover, the law also provides a liberty to the plaintiff to act upon a mere threat of violation of legal rights even when the injury isn't completely caused under the provisions of Special Relief Act.

Dissection of definition-

Injuria sine damnum literally means injury without damage.

- Injuria means legal injury. It means infringement of a legal right an individual possesses in a democratic country.
- Sine means without.
- Damnum means damage. It refers to any harm, mischief or misfortune inflicted on another person or her property.

Illustration

If A wrongfully detains B by locking him in a room without any lawful reason, there is a violation of the B's legal right. The maxim of injuria sine damnum is applicable in this instance. According to this principle, B is entitled to claim substantial damages to compensate for the wrongful imprisonment even if no damage was suffered by him.

In brief, the maxim of injuria sine damnum provides remedy against many types of damages.

CASE LAWS TO ILLUSTRATE INJURIA SINE DAMNO

1. Bhim Singh vs. State of J. & K [2]

FACTS:

In the case of Bhim Singh vs. State of J. & K [2], the plaintiff was a Jammu & Kashmir MLA, on the way to the assembly session and the police unreasonably detained him. He was also not presented before a magistrate[5]

HELD:

Since his fundamental right[6] was infringed with, the law awarded him compensation of Rs. 50,000 on the basis of injuria sine damnum.

2. Ashby v White[7]

In the case of Ashby v White, the claimant was a qualified voter at an election. The defendant who was a returning officer wrongfully refused to take the vote of the plaintiff. The wronged party suffered no damage since the candidate whom he wished to vote already won the election, but still the defendant was held guilty by the court because of unreasonable infringement of the legal right to vote of the claimant.

3. Sain Das Vs. Ujagar Singh (1940) [8]

It was cited in this case that injuria sine damnum applies in the cases of trespass as well. Injuria sine damnum is applicable in cases wherein there is an unlawful intrusion in someone's property without any reason. In these cases, nominal damages are awarded to the aggrieved.

DAMNUM SINE INJURIA

Damnum sine injuria literally means "damage or harm without legal injury." In this, there is a damage suffered by the plaintiff without interference with the individual's legal rights. Since there is no violation of the rights vested by the law, no action can be taken in respect to damnum sine injuria. Damages can be in the form of loss suffered in terms of money, property, health etc.

CASE LAWS TO ILLUSTRATE INJURIA SINE DAMNUM

1. Gloucester Grammar School's Case (1410) YB 11 Hen IV, fo. pl. 201, 23

FACTS:

In the case of Gloucester Grammar School (1410), a schoolmaster sets up a rival school beside the school of the complainant. Due to this, the plaintiff suffered a significant loss because of reduction in fees. [9]

HELD:

The court ruled that since no legal right was infringed with, no liability can be imposed on the defendant and no compensation will be awarded to the plaintiff.

2. Mogul Steamship Co. v. McGregor Gow and Co.[10]

FACTS:

A number of steamship companies combined together and drove the plaintiff company out of the tea-carrying trade by offering reduced freight.

HELD:

The House of Lords held that the plaintiff had no cause of action as the defendants had by lawful means acted to protect and extend their trade and increase their profits.

3. Om Saran v Sub-Divisional Magistrate, Chandausi, Moradabad and Another

FACTS:

Petitioner, a licence holder of petty diesel dealer in village Majhole District Moradabad, has filed this writ petition challenging the advertisement for grant of another licence published in a newspaper, for the same village.

His grievances that the demand of diesel is not such so as to require grant of additional licence for the sale of diesel, and if such a licence is granted it will cripple his business.

HELD:

The Court held that 'The letter is from the Government to all the District Magistrates of this State, whereby guidelines for granting licence of petty diesel dealer, have been laid down. The petitioner cannot enforce those guidelines. It is a matter between the Government and its District Magistrates. This letter does not confer any right on the petitioner so as to challenge the grant of new licence to other person.'

MORAL WRONGS

Damnum sine injuria comes under moral wrongs. It is a wide-accepted principle that there are no remedies in case of moral wrongs. This is subject to the condition that no legal rights have been bypassed.

CASE LAW TO ILLUSTRATE MORAL WRONG

Mayor & Co. of Bradford vs. Pickles (1895)

FACTS:

As in the case of Mayor & Co. of Bradford vs. Pickles (1895), a suit was filed against Mayor & Co. by Bradford Co., asserting that the defendant had dug a well in the adjoining land owned by the plaintiff which had stopped the underground supply of water to the corporation, causing them huge financial losses due to inadequate water supply for citizens living in their jurisdiction. [11]

HELD:

It was governed that the defendant is not liable since there was no violation of legal rights.

CONCLUSION

It can be concluded that legal damage refers to an infringement of rights granted to individuals by the law. It can refer to damage to property or body. Taking the example of trespass, if A enters the property of B without causing harm to the property, it is an actionable per se crime since the legal right [12] of the plaintiff has been violated.

The tort law is also based on the maxim *ubi jus ibi remedium* which means- where there's a right, there's a remedy[13]. This right to remedy is a universally hailed right, accepted by majority of the legal systems. The law hence provides remedies to all sorts of wrongs that are committed.

Injury can be caused either by negligent or malicious action. The main difference between the two is of intention. In a negligence-caused injury, the tort-feasor unintentionally harms the plaintiff. For example, while having an argument with a friend, if they smash a cup on the floor and a shard strikes your eye, the friend has committed a tort but it is an act of negligence since it was unintentional. Meanwhile, if while having an argument, the friend throws a cup at you, injuring you, intentionally, a tort has been committed of battery.

There are two types of injuries encapsulated in the two maxims, as discussed, injuria sine damnum and damnum sine injuria. From these two, injuria sine damnum is actionable per se (harm does not need to be proven) since it violates the legal rights of an individual. This maxim says that the infringement of an individual's legal right itself constitutes a damage and the corresponding actual damage need not be proven in the court.

Injuria sine damnum and its counterpart, damnum sine injuria form the very basis of the concept of damages in the world around us. We can say that this duo is the very bedrock of the various remedies available against a plethora of wrongs. Talking about the subject of this article, injuria sine damnum is the bigger of the two because the affected can claim damages against it. It suggests that the infringement of a legal right is much grave than the damage caused to a person. This damage however should be the consequence of a legal action. A greater focus is laid upon compensating the plaintiff rather than punishing the wrongdoer.

This concept was developed in early times to provide a method that all the courts could follow in various contexts to bring the aggrieved party back to its original position before any harm was done to them.

At the very root, law means justice and fairness. Every wrong action has a consequence on an innocent and the wrongdoer is compelled by the law to compensate the affected party.

References:

[1] Winfield and Jolowicz, Tort (11th ed. By W.V.H. Rogers) 3 (1979)

[2] Legal Information Institute, Tort LII / Legal Information Institute (2017), https://www.law.cornell.edu/wex/tort.

[3] Diva Rai, Constituents of Tort and the Tortious Liability Equation iPleaders (2019), https://blog.ipleaders.in/what-constitutes-a-tort/ (last visited Nov 7, 2021).

[4] Holt, C.J, Ashby v. White (1703) 2 Lord Rayam 938

[5] The Constitution of India, Art 22(2)

[6] The Constitution of India, Art 21

[7] (1703) 92 ER 126

[8] (1940) ILR21LAH191

[9] Gloucester Grammar School's Case (1410) YB 11 Hen IV, fo. pl. 201, 23

[10] (1893) A.C. 25

[11] Alan Roseland, The Mayor of Bradford v Pickles Case Brief Wiki (2019), https://casebrief.fandom.com/wiki/The_Mayor_of_Bradford_v_Pickles

[12] Constitution of India, Art 21

[13] Saumya Saxena, Ubi jus ibi remedium: where there is a right, there is a remedy iPleaders (2019), https://blog.ipleaders.in/ubi-jus-ibi-remedium/

CHAPTER THREE

A Study on Occupational Hazards and Health of Labourers of Leather Industries in Tamil Nadu, with Special Reference to Vellore District

Megha Mahesh*

**Student, School of Excellence in Law*

INTRODUCTION:

Workers often sustain an injury or contract a disease arising out of their employment for which the employer and worker's compensation insurer deny worker's compensation benefits, on the grounds that the worker cannot identify a specific traumatic event that caused or precipitated the injury or disease. Such a denial may be contrary to fact and law. It is not always necessary for the worker to be able to identify a specific event or date of injury for the claim to be compensable.

A person who works in a coal mine, cement factory, foundry, or motor vehicle manufacturing plant, and as a result of the dirty, dusty, oily air, contracts a lung disease would never be able to identify a specific traumatic event that caused the condition, or a specific date of injury or disease. A person who works over a long period of time performing heavy physical labor in the construction industry, manufacturing industry, or other material handling industry, and as a result of heavy lifting contracts a pathologic condition of the neck, back, shoulder, hip or knee may not be able, with any degree of certainty, to identify a specific traumatic event that caused the condition, or a specific date of injury or disease. Even a sedentary person who works at a computer, in assembly, or any other occupation requiring repetitive hand movements, and a result contracts carpal tunnel syndrome, cannot with any degree of certainty identify a specific traumatic event that caused the condition, or a specific date of injury or disease.

The leather industry occupies a place of eminence in the Indian economy because of its massive potential for employment, growth, and exports. The industry has received criticism on environmental grounds, and the tanning industry viewed to be a major source of water pollution.[1] Tannery occupation is known for the pollutant, having health risks at the workplace. Due to this, the working environment plays important health risk factors among tannery workers. Working in tanneries exposed tannery workers to physical, chemical, and biological agents as well environment, which makes them vulnerable to several toxic chemicals, which are hazardous for health and might lead to an increase in morbidity and mortality.[2] The chemical hazards in tanneries include vegetal tannins, chromium salts, and biocides, bleaching agents, hydrogen sulphide, and dyes. Infection with anthrax is common. The hazards may cause minor illnesses, or they may lead to severe chronic debilitating diseases.[3] Dust produced by various processes such as by buffing and shaving and this dust can affect the respiratory tract, leading to the most common respiratory problem of chronic bronchitis among the tannery workers.[4] Similarly, Chromium produced in tanneries has the potential to bind with skin proteins of tannery workers to produce complex antigens, which lead to hypersensitivity. The resulting contact dermatitis could be a preliminary condition to the development of bronchial asthma.[5][6] Chromium dust may enter the body by inhalation, ingestion, and by direct cutaneous contact. Exposure to Chromium increases the risk of dermatitis, ulcers, and perforation of the nasal septum and respiratory illnesses along with increased lung and nasal cancers.[7] Chromium-specific health hazards like carcinoma of the larynx and lung parenchyma and paranasal sinuses have also been reported.[8] There are very limited studies of the health effects of chronic exposure to chromium in leather tanning among developing countries. In India, it was reported previously about varying prevalence of asthma among leather tannery workers with moderate to high exposures at the workplace to be significantly associated with asthma. There is a further need to study prevalence and risk factors of Asthma, Tuberculosis, and Chronic bronchitis in tannery workers to better account for Asthma burden and to identify high-risk exposures in a factory environment for prevention purposes. This study intended to estimate the prevalence of asthma, tuberculosis, and chronic bronchitis among leather tannery workers and to identify the risk factors associated with it in Vellore District, India.

Data and methods

This cross sectional household study was conducted during the period January–June 2015 among male tannery and non-tannery workers in the Jajmau area of Vellore District in the state of Tamilnadu, India.

Status of leather industries in Tamilnadu- Tamil Nadu is India's leader in leather with around 60 % share in the country's tanning capacity and finished leather production. About 6 % of the global finished leather supply is manufactured in this state. Leather production in Tamil Nadu ranges from preparing rawhides for tanning to the production of the finished leather to the production of 'wet blue' (raw chrome-tanned hides) and it provided employment to more than 100,000 people in 2008-2009, with consistent growth over the last years. Vaniyambadi and Ambur, two cities in the Vellore district, are the main centers of leather and leather products manufacturing in the state. In Ambur, 102 tanning units are registered under the Factories Act. According to the Vaniyambadi Tanners Association, 90% of the units in the Ambur cluster are export-oriented and production in Vaniyambadi is exclusively for export. Tamilnadu is the only state that enforced Zero Liquid Discharge on leather processing units. 53% of the leather industries of India are located in Tamilnadu and Vellore district houses major leather industries in Tamilnadu. The major production centers of leather and leather productions in the state are Chennai, Ambur, Ranipet, Vanniyambadi, Perambur, Tiruchirapalli, and Dindigul. The contribution of the district Vellore in the GDP of Tamil Nadu is significant and is one of the top 10 contributors to the GDP of the State, it contributes USD 3.8 billion in the GDP of Tamil Nadu. Vellore district itself accounts for more than 37% of the country's leather export. In the past few years with around 3000 industrial units established with an investment of $ 51 Million. . Some of the prominent MSME clusters are leather, textile, and handloom & safety match industries. The district also has 12 large-scale and 300 medium-scale industries and the majority of them are engaged in leather production. The Vellore District has a dominant presence in the Leather and leather-based industries. It accounts for more than 37% of the country's export leather and leather-related products. Even though many large scale industries like BHEL, EID Parry, Tirumalai Chemicals and Greaves, SAME-DEUTZ, TVS–Brakes India, Mitsubishi, Greaves Cotton, MRF, Kramski Stamping and Molding India Pvt Ltd., RSL Industries Ltd, Farida Shoes Ltd, etc are functioning, there are 12,396 micro and small Enterprises functioning in Vellore District and a majority of them are being engaged in leather processing is thrashed with the entire district of Vellore.

ISSUES IDENTIFIED PERTAINING TO OCCUPATIONAL AND HEALTH HAZARDS AMONG LABORERS OF LEATHER INDUSTRIES IN THE VELLORE DISTRICT

1. The Ecological Challenges- The workers of the leather industries are the immediate victims of the changing atmosphere and the most dangerous part of modern tanning is handling chromium, which causes a myriad of ailments depending on how it is absorbed. If it merges with the respiratory systems of our body, it acts as a lung irritant and carcinogen, affecting the upper respiratory tract, obstructing airways, and increasing the chances of

developing lung, nasal, or sinus cancer. The tanning industries in Ambur, Vaniyampadi, Pernampet, and Ranipet of the Vellore District lead to both the environment of these areas and respiratory problems to those who are working. The primary environmental threat involves the dumping of solid and liquid waste that contains leftover chromium and other hazardous compounds. 40% of tannery workers in this district have health problems because they are in direct contact with chemicals.

2. Groundwater contamination due to effluent from the leather industry- Groundwater contamination is prevalent in Vellore District due to the excessive number of leather industries in the district. The process being undertaken by the leather industries leads to huge consumption of water along with dangerous chemicals like lime, sodium carbonate, sodium bicarbonate, common salt, sodium sulfate, chrome sulfate, fats, oils, dyes, etc. Contaminations of the groundwater lead to the availability of unhealthy drinking water, a limited quantity of water availability land other health issues. In addition to this, it is very sad that the existence of the river Palar has become questionable because of water pollution by a cluster of tanneries which are distributed along its banks. Tannery industries in Tamil Nadu concentrated more than 70% tanneries are located in Ranipet, Vanaiyambadi, Dindigul, Ambur. This industry is one of the major consumers of fresh water and most of the water is discharged as wastewater. The quantity of total wastewater discharged for 100 kg of skins and hides processed varies from 3000 to 3200 liters. Common salt is the biggest polluting material in the tanning industry. The amount of wastewater generated by the tanneries is approximately from 2.5 to 3.0 million liters per day, which is, in turn, is collected in irrigation lakes. According to a report, a sole tannery is capable of causing the pollution of groundwater in scope of about 7 to 8 km in radius. The pollution from tanneries has caused irrevocable deterioration of the quality of groundwater in the vast areas. Hence proper water treatment is required in terms of community health.
3. Growth of a large number of unorganized & unregulated leather tanneries- Due to unorganized and unregulated leather tanneries contamination of groundwater due to large discharge of wastewater has become un-controllable.
4. Occupational hazards/ deaths- An estimated 2.78 million workers die per year as a result of occupational accidents or work-related diseases, this adds three trillion dollars of the annual cost to the global economy Occupational deaths in India in the year 2011 was 3,87,857 people (45/hour) (Yadav, 2019), and that mortality was due to Communicable diseases, Cancers, Respiratory Diseases, Circulatory diseases, Mental Disorders, Digestive systems diseases, Genitourinary system, Accidents, and violence. This is an indication of how vulnerable are the working groups to occupational health in India across sectors. The survey in Tamilnadu indicates that around 78% of workers were affected by health problems. Majority of the workers were affected with Musculoskeletal disorder(31.7%) and others problems including Skin problem(15.7%), Respiratory problem(16.9%), Eye problem(6.5%), Ear problem(0.4%), Dental problem(2.6%), C.N.S problem(0.4%), C.V.S problem(0.9%), Abdomen problem(2.6%) and Uro-Genital problem(0.4%). There was an association between certain factors like Gender, Occupation, Nourishment, past history of illness with the morbidities among the leather workers.
5. Child Labour in the leather industry- There are several examples of children found at work in Indian tanneries under inhuman conditions, forced to work more than 12 hours a day. In the tanneries in the region around Tamil Nadu boys aged 11 or 12 are employed to clean the tanning tumblers since they can easily climb inside the chambers.53 In February 2015, hundreds of children were rescued from leather units in Hyderabad, who were kept in unhygienic and unventilated dark rooms monitored by video cameras, many suffering from skin problems and other diseases. Similar rescue operations have taken place in many other leather production centers in India.

Supreme Court judgment pertaining to occupational health: The Petitioner from a non-profit occupational health and safety organization, registered under the Societies Registration Act, 1860, has invoked the extra-ordinary jurisdiction of this Court under Article 32 of the Constitution of India seeking for reliefs primarily to issue a writ of mandamus or any other appropriate writ, order, or direction directing the Respondents to frame guidelines with respect to occupational safety and health regulations to be maintained by various industries. The petitioner highlighted the serious diseases, the workers working in thermal plants are suffering from over a period of years, the report also indicated that half of the workers have lung function abnormalities, pulmonary function test abnormalities, senor neuro loss, skin diseases, asthma, etc. Referring to the same, the court passed an interim order on 30.1.2008, to reduce the occupational hazards of the employees working in various thermal power stations in the country after taking note of the various suggestions made (Supreme Court of India, 2008).

2. Supreme Court of India in Vellore Citizens Welfare Forum vs Union Of India & others- It was a public interest - under Article 32 of the Constitution of India has been filed by Vellore Citizens Welfare Forum and is directed against the pollution which is being caused by an enormous discharge of untreated effluent by the tanneries and other industries in the State of Tamil Nadu. The SC directed the Chief Justice of the Madras High Court to constitute a special Bench "Green bench" as already functioning at Calcutta, Madhya Pradesh, and some other High Courts to deal with this case and other environmental matters and it would be open to the Bench to pass any appropriate order/ orders keeping in view the directions issued by the SC.

Applicability of The Employees Compensation Act 1923-

Occupational Disease

An occupational disease is a compensable condition under Wisconsin worker's compensation law. Specifically, it is identified in the Worker's Compensation Act of Wisconsin under the definition of "injury" in §102.01(c) as follows; "'Injury' means mental or physical harm to an employee caused by accident or disease." In this context, the word "disease" is used to represent the types of injuries, disabilities, or conditions that are not the result of a singular accident or trauma. Occupational diseases are not as easily recognized as accidental injuries. For example, an employee may fracture an arm or tear a ligament if something falls on him at work. This type of injury is considered an accidental injury and establishes an accurate date of injury and causation. These factors are not so explicit in an occupational disease case.[9]

To be eligible for the Employees' Compensation Act's benefits there are some requirements that need to be fulfilled:

1. You must be an employee of the Company or Organisation.
2. You must have been injured at the workplace or the job was as such that you have been injured.

Section 3: Employer's liability for Compensation

Employer's liability in case of occupational diseases

There are certain occupations which expose employees to particular diseases that are inherent-

- Infra-red radiations;
- Skin diseases due to chemical or leather processing units;
- Hearing impairment caused by noise;
- Lung cancer caused by asbestos dust and Diseases due to effect of extreme climatic conditions.

Example- Miners are at a risk of developing a disease called silicosis. Sometimes miners also develop lung diseases due to exposure to dust. The people who work in agricultural lands, develop diseases through spraying of pesticides. These pesticides are toxic in nature and are health hazards to many farmers.[10]

There are thousands of workplaces where occupation itself is dangerous in nature.

Provided that the employer shall not be liable:

(a) if any injury does not result in the total or partial disablement of the employee for a period exceeding three days;

(b) if any injury does not result in death or permanent total disablement caused by an accident which is directly attributable to-

- if the employee is under the influence of drink or drugs at that time,
- the willful disobedience of the employee to an order expressly given, or to a rule expressly framed, for the purpose of securing the safety of employees,

- the wilful removal by the employee of any safety guard or other devices which he knew to have been provided for the purpose of securing the safety of employees.

The Act provides that compensation is provided to employees and their dependants only if the injuries from the accident include occupational diseases. The accident must occur in the course of employment the Act also applies to railway servants and persons employed in any such capacity as specified in Schedule 2 of the Employees Compensation Act. The people employed in factories, mines, plantations, vehicles, construction works, and certain other hazardous occupations come under Schedule 2.

Part A of Schedule III

If an employee contracts any disease that is mentioned in occupational diseases or the employee is employed for a continuous period of six months (this does not include the service period) and not less than that, the employer shall not be liable to pay the compensation as the disease will be deemed to be injury and it shall be considered as out of course of employment.

Part B of Schedule III

1. Diseases caused by phosphorus or the toxic substance present, all include exposure to risk concerned.
2. Diseases caused by mercury or toxic substances found exposure to the risk concerned.
3. Diseases caused by benzene or the toxic substances found which pose risk to the concerned.
4. Diseases caused by nitro and amino toxic substances of benzene involve risk to the concerned.

These diseases are considered occupational diseases, and they are deemed to be out of the course of employment and therefore the employer will not be liable to pay the compensation.

Part C of Schedule III

If an employee contracts a disease that is mentioned as an occupational disease which is specific to that employment, during a continuous period that is less than the period mentioned under this part of Schedule 3 is known as occupational diseases. It will be deemed that the disease has arisen out of and in the course of the employment, the contracting of such disease will be deemed to be an injury by accident within the meaning of this Section

Pneumoconiosis is a disease caused by sclerogenic mineral dust (silicosis, anthracosilicosis, asbestosis) and silico-tuberculosis if silicosis is an essential factor in causing the resultant incapacity or death, such diseases are considered as occupational diseases.

Section 3(4)

No compensation will be payable to an employee unless the disease is directly attributable to a specific injury that arises out of or in the course of employment.

Arising out of and in the course of employment- Three factors determine whether the act is arising out of or in the course of employment:

- When the injury occurred, the employee must have been engaged in the business of the employer. Also, he must not be doing something for his benefit. The accident must occur where the employer was performing his duties.
- The injuries occurred because of the risk incidental to the duties of the work or services or if the nature or condition of employment is inherent.
- Notional extension of Employer's Premises. When there is a causal connection between the accident and the place where the employee is working, compensation is payable for the disability or death of the person according to the Employees Compensation Act. This is the Doctrine of Notional Extension of the workplace.[11][12]

Section 4: Amount of compensation, Where death results from the injury- In case the employee dies, an amount equal to fifty percent of the monthly wages multiplied by a factor as given in Schedule 4 of the act or rupees eighty thousand is given whichever is more.

Where permanent total disablement results from the injury- In case the employee has total disablement the amount given is sixty percent or rupees ninety thousand whichever is more.

Where permanent partial disablement results from injury- In the case of permanent partial disablement, the compensation provided is equal to disability as sixty percent or rupees ninety thousand.

Liability of Insurer- The liability of the insurer is determined based on the wages of the employee. The number of wages are covered under the insurance policy. The company will be liable to indemnify only that portion of the amount which is under wages.

Causal connection between disease and occupation- The amount of compensation is paid when the insurer certifies that the injury is the result of an occupational disease.

THE OCCUPATIONAL SAFETY, HEALTH, AND WORKING CONDITIONS CODE, 2020

An Act to consolidate and amend the laws regulating the occupational safety, health, and working conditions of the persons employed in an establishment and for matters connected therewith or incidental thereto.

CONCLUSION -

Any development without the health of the community is not acceptable. Any kind of industrial or economic growth after victimizing the life of the public will not provide any fortune to the nation. Therefore, we must understand that such kind of contamination is creating cascade effects on the present, Water recycling units with the most modern technology are needed to replace the present traditional water recycling units, which consume more chromium and other chemicals.

References:

[1] S.P. Singh

Health hazards among workers of leather industries in unnao district- A statistical review International Journal of Current Engineering and Scientific Research (Ijcesr), Vol 4 (10) (2017) 2393-8374

[2] A. Jamal, A. Mehmood, T. Putus, H. Savolainen, J. Liesivuori, *et al.*, Prevalence of respiratory symptoms, bronchial asthma and obstructive lung disease among tannery workers, Ann Environ Sci Toxicol, 2 (1) (2017), pp. 33-42, 10.17352/aest.000010

[3] R.B. Raidas, Occupational health hazards in tanneries. Directorate general factory advice service & labour institutes, Mumbai, India Indoshnews, 2 (2007), pp. 4-7

[4] https://www.sciencedirect.com/science/article/pii/S221339842030172X#bib3

[5] L.E. Lockman, Case report: allergic contact dermatitis and new-onset asthma. Chromium exposure during leather tanning, Can Fam Physician, 48 (2002), p. 1907

[6] K. Shahzad, S. Akhtar, S. Mahmud

Prevalence and determinants of asthma in adult male leather tannery workers in Karachi, Pakistan: a cross sectional study, BMC Publ Health, 6 (1) (2006), p. 292

[7] D. Basketter, L. Horev, D. Slodovnik, S. Merimes, A. Trattner, A. Ingber Investigation of the threshold for allergic reactivity to chromium. Contact Dermatitis, 44 (2001), pp. 70-74

[8] S.K. Rastogi, C. Kesavchandran, F. Mahdi, A. Panday- Occupational cancers in leather tanning industries: a short review, Indian J Occup Environ Med, 11 (2007), pp. 3-5

[9] Zabkowicz v. Industrial Comm. 264 Wis. 317, 322, 58 N.W.2d 677 (1953)

[10] Rathjen v. Industrial Comm., 233 Wis. 452, 460, 29 N.W. 618 (1940)

[11]N.A. Chauhan v. N.K. Shah 1991 ACJ 904, (1991) 1 GLR 361, (1993) IIILLJ 611 Guj

[12]Moondra & Co. V/s Mst. Bhawani AIR 1970 Raj 111

CHAPTER FOUR

A Critical Analysis of Post-Mortem Examination

Nishtha Vaswani*

**4th Year, BA LLB, Symbiosis Law School, Hyderabad*

INTRODUCTION

Post-mortem and autopsy are words of quotidian nature to people related to a criminal investigation or medical field. Although, the other public has a general idea about the same, the in-depth knowledge and procedures for performing it are still vague to people who are alien to criminal investigation and the medical field. The meaning perceived by common people is, when a person dies and the body goes for examination to a medical practitioner then it is called post-mortem examination or an autopsy.[1] Autopsy originated from an ancient word, "*Autopsia*" which is derived from "*Autos*" meaning "oneself" and "*Opsis*" i.e. "to see for oneself".[2] The post-mortem is a Latin word and according to Webster Law Dictionary means, "after death. Generally used to refer to the examination of a corpse by the coroner to ascertain cause of death".[3] The same dictionary defines autopsy as, "the post-mortem examination of a human body, including its dissection and the removal of inspection of the major organs, to determine the cause of death."[4] These definitions show that though autopsy and a post-mortem examination are connoted similar, there is a slight difference between the two, and post-mortem examination is a wider term than an autopsy. In the post-mortem, the body of the deceased need not necessarily be internally examined to know the cause of death unlike in autopsy the major organs are examined by dissection.

There are various types of post-mortems, one of which is forensic post-mortem. It is performed in cases where legal action is required on the death of a person, if the death is unnatural or the cause of death is not ascertained, etc. A person can die at any time during day or night, but can the body be examined in artificial light if the deceased passes away post-sunset. In India, different states have different guidelines for performing post-mortem in artificial light, with certain conditions. This aspect of night post-mortems is discussed in detail under Chapter 2 of this research paper.

Autopsy or post-mortem examination can only be performed by medical officers who are bound by legal technicalities, but how much do they adhere to it, is the major contention. Thus, this paper intends to provide an overview of the post-mortem examination, its types, ways to perform it, etc. This paper majorly will highlight the critical analysis of the behavior of medical practitioners during performing post-mortem examination as discussed in various judgments, the procedures which are provided by the legislature for post-mortem examination in India, and to what extent they are practically implemented by the officers and practitioners involved in conducting such examination.

POST-MORTEM: TYPES AND REASONS

Pathologists suffered and had hurdles in performing autopsies as the dead bodies were considered "unclean" and thus pathologists faced the "beetles of sinister aspect" because of religious beliefs, this was mentioned by Major DP Lambert in 1938.[5] There is still a certain fraction of the population who do not support post-mortem examination because of religious factors.[6] Thus, medical examiners are obliged to conduct post-mortem examinations with care and caution by following the legal requirements. A post-mortem examination is done for clinical, academic, and medico-legal (forensic) purposes.[7] Medical students anatomize dead bodies to study various external and internal organs, and structures of the human body, this is called academic post-mortem examination.[8] Pathologists or clinicians perform post-mortem to identify the cause of death in cases wherein either during the treatment the diagnosis could not be reached or the same was doubtful, this is called pathological or clinical post-mortem.[9] A clinical and academic post-mortem is performed with the consent of the deceased's relatives.[10] In the forensic post-mortem, cranial, thoracic, and abdominal cavities are opened up whereas in pathological post-mortem only the area infected with the disease may be examined.[11]

There are various reasons to perform post-mortem examination, like to know the reason of death, manner of death, approximate time of death, identify the person, was deceased suffering from any disease, etc.[12] Evidently, a post-mortem is performed to ascertain the cause of death, this lays a vital responsibility on the shoulders of the medical officer performing it, especially in cases of infanticide. The witnesses are limited in such cases who have seen the child alive and breathing. The primary witness is the pathologist who conducts the post-mortem as he would provide the information to the court that whether the infant was born dead or he died after birth. The complex aspect is proving the separate existence of the infant from the mother.[13] If the case of infanticide is on the mother, then the pathologist must prove in his findings that the death of the infant was deliberated by the mother or was an omission on her part, and the infant had a separate existence from the mother when it died.[14]

In certain periods autopsies were considered to be a quotidian work, however with the passing time and development of law, the restrictions and punishments for negligence increased, consequently, the rate of mandatory autopsies declined.[15] There are certain conditions, circumstances, and crimes prescribed, in which post-mortem examination can be done.[16] Since courts give more weightage to medical evidence than ordinary evidence, it becomes necessary to investigate even small details with complete care and caution.[17]

PROCEDURE UNDER INDIAN LEGISLATION

Section 174 and 176 of the Criminal Procedure Code (CrPC) mention inquiry into the cause of death and other circumstances by either Police or Magistrate or Court.[18] The Medico-legal autopsy which is given implicitly in the said sections of CrPC is conducted when a doctor is not able to give a death certificate or when the death is believed to be unnatural.[19] The forensic or medico-legal post-mortem is conducted on-demand from law officers in circumstances of sudden, obscure, unnatural, or litigious deaths. Such law officers are generally police officers not below the rank of sub-inspector or executive magistrate who are indulged in the investigation of such death criminal cases.[20] The medical officer, if directed to perform a post-mortem, cannot waive off such duty and has to comply with the instructions of the law officer who has directed for post-mortem.[21] The medical officer must take into account the ascertained cause of death by the investigators in case of post-mortem of a decomposed body to understand the suspected organ or area of the body which might give a clue about the cause of death.[22] The three cavities when opened during forensic post-mortem may reveal the cause of death, but to avoid any doubtful interrogative repercussions in court, the whole body must be examined by the medical officer as partial post-mortem is not permissible under the Indian legislations.[23] If he is called upon as an expert witness in the court of law, as per section 45 of the Indian Evidence Act, 1872, then it will be easier for him to explain the medical position of the deceased if his opinion is required by the court.

The performance of night post-mortems is another bone of contention and a controversial one. It is generally advised by experts to perform post-mortem under daylight as there are contradictions in the appearance of the colour of injuries in daylight and artificial light.[24] However, in India, some states have allowed performing post-mortems at night by provided that the conditions mentioned in guidelines are fulfilled by the medical practitioners. The Gujarat government lays restriction on night post-mortems if there's a case of poisoning if the case is of women below thirty years of age if the deceased is a woman who died at her husband's or in-law's place, if the body is distorted and if sufficient light resembling daylight is not present.[25] The Kerala and Maharashtra government does not do not lay any restriction on performing night post-mortems, the latter however instructed that presence of adequate quantity and quality of light must be present resembling the daylight.[26] In 1996, the Tamilnadu government permitted night post-mortems to be performed in government hospitals, if the claimants of the deceased insisted and the death occurred in an accident.[27] However, there were not adequate facilities available to perform post-mortem at night and the said order was stayed by the Madras High Court in the case of **K Mathiharan v. State of TN Represented by its Secretary, Department of Health and Family Welfare**[28]. Hence, the order was modified and currently, the post-mortem can be performed from 6 AM to 6 PM in Tamilnadu.[29] There are certain arguments against night post-mortems, the major one being that a large number of the Indian population has dark-toned skin which makes it difficult in night time for injuries to be identified as it would camouflage with the skin and perhaps leading to an important injury being missed.[30]

These are certain aspects that are important to keep in mind while performing post-mortems, which is the provisions under which forensic post-mortem is permitted and whether the respective state allows to perform post-mortem when the body is sent for such examination by law officers. Also, it must be ensured by the medical officer that when he prepares the post-mortem report, such must not be very technical and easy to understand by the court and other authorities involved in the case.

IMPORTANT CASES

The pathologists conducting the post-mortem have the duty to lay out the findings which are important for the court to deliver a judgment when such post-mortem is in consideration as a piece of vital evidence in cases of homicidal or accidental deaths. However, there have been certain cases wherein the medical practitioner was in default by not conducting the post-mortem properly and hence such findings were not considered by the court while such medical practitioners were charged and disciplinary action against them was ordered by the court. Some of the cases are discussed below which deal with negligence of medical officers while conducting a post-mortem and few other controversial aspects of post-mortem examination under Indian legislation.

In the case of **Gudar Dusadh v. State of Bihar**[31], the Supreme Court relied heavily on post-mortem reports and medical expert opinion regarding the same to ascertain the objective liability. The issue before the court was whether the offense was murder or culpable homicide not amounting to murder. While referring to the post-mortem report of the deceased prepared by Dr. R.S. Singh, it was stated that a lacerated deep wound was found on the left side of the head. Further, according to Dr. Singh, the cause of death of the deceased was compression on the left side of the brain, and such injury in the ordinary course could lead to the death of a person. The court admitted the opinion of Dr. Singh and held the injury was adequate to cause death in the ordinary course and resulted in the death of the deceased. Such reliance on post-mortem reflects that if there is sufficient evidence to support the post-mortem then it holds a heavy evidentiary value. Similarly, in the case of **Pulicherla Nagaraju v. State of Andhra Pradesh**[32], wherein a dangerous weapon called Barisa was used to kill the deceased. The deceased had no weapons, was unarmed. There was the absence of provocation or sudden fight, there was the previous enmity. The deceased according to the post-mortem report was stabbed with a high force that was sufficient in the ordinary course to kill someone. Further, the report mentioned that "...deceased would appear to have died due to haemorrhage and shock due to injuries to right sub-clavier artery and upper lobe of right lung." The Supreme Court was satisfied that the incident could not be covered under the exception to murder relying on the circumstances and post-mortem report and hence did not interfere in the conviction judgment passed by the High Court.

The Supreme Court in the case of **Mohd. Zahid v. State of Tamil Nadu**[33]examined the validity of expert opinion, and observed that the medical officer who conducts the post-mortem, while presenting his evidence in court, must produce sufficient authority in support of his opinion. Otherwise, his opinion would not be considered to convict an accused based upon his post-mortem report. This observation reflects that an expert opinion concerning the post-mortem report will carry no evidentiary value in absence of substantive authority to support the report.

In the case of **Dayal Singh and Ors. v. State of Uttaranchal**[34], the deceased, his wife, and their two children were injured. Dr. P. C. Pande examined them at the Public Health Centre of Sittarganj and injuries of all of them including deceased, Dayal Singh. Three visible injuries were recorded by Dr. Pande on the body of the deceased. The body was sent for post-mortem and Dr. C. N. Tiwari conducted it. According to Dr. Tiwari, there were no external or internal injuries on the body of the deceased, this statement conflicted with statements of all other witnesses who mentioned that the accused had come with Lathi to beat the deceased, and the presence of three visible injuries on the body of the deceased. The Supreme Court framed the issue, "Whenever there is some conflict in the eye-witness version of events and the medical evidence, what effect will it have on the case of the prosecution and what would be the manner in which the Court should appreciate such evidence?" The court did not rely on the report of Dr. Tiwari and further directed the respective authorities to take disciplinary action against him irrespective of him being retired or on service because the report prepared was in contradiction with the inquest report and other reliable witnesses, and such was an intentional dereliction on part of Dr. Tiwari. This judgment has given an essential and strong decision against the medical practitioner who involves themselves in tampering with the reports, etc.

The Supreme Court in the case of **In Re: To Issue Certain Guidelines Regarding Inadequacies and Deficiencies in Criminal Trials v. The State of Andhra Pradesh and Ors.**[35], deliberated upon the Draft Rules of Criminal Practice, 2021 and issued direction recently on 20th April 2021, for incorporating the same by all High Courts within a period of six months from the date of judgment and acquiring the requisite approvals or cooperation, if required from the State government within the same time period. Further, the court directed the State governments and the Union of India to incorporate the changes required in police manuals and issue consequential required guidelines within six months from the date of this judgment. This draft rules under Chapter I titled Investigation contains rules regarding post-mortem which requires every post-mortem report to carry on the backside a printed format of the human body, both frontal and rearview, and injuries if there are any, to be mentioned on such sketch. In the cases of death in police action or police custody, the magistrate or the investigating officer shall ask the hospital or the medical practitioner to arrange the photos or videography while performing post-mortem along with the photos of the deceased. Such photography or videography shall be performed by a police photographer or nominated photographer by the state government, and if both are absent a private photographer may be engaged. The photos and videos are to be presented as evidence during the trial and proper procedure under the Indian Evidence Act needs to be followed. This step taken by the court will somehow affect the procedures currently present and will enhance the accountability of both investigating and medical officers.

SUGGESTIONS

The following are few suggestions presented after studying certain aspects of medico-legal post-mortems in India:

- There is a need to have a common regulation for performing post-mortem at night time.
- The evidentiary value of the post-mortem report must be placed equivalent with the other witnesses if there are any because the medical technology has not evolved much to give 100% sure results.
- The benefit of the doubt based on a post-mortem report must only be given if there is other corroborative evidence.
- The medical practitioner performing post-mortem must have a clear record of his career and such must be ensured by the court.

CONCLUSION

The post-mortem examination comes into the picture only in criminal cases, specifically in the cases of homicide or accident where a person dies. The legislation concerning central criminal laws in India is covered under the Criminal Procedure Code, Indian Penal Code, and Indian Evidence Act. All the three legislations are quite extensive, however have no mention of the post-mortem reports explicitly. Different states in India have different guidelines for conducting post-mortems, there is no uniformity. There is a need to bring uniformity as it will leave out the places of doubt. The judgment in the case of In Re: To Issue Certain Guidelines Regarding Inadequacies and Deficiencies in Criminal Trials v. The State of Andhra Pradesh and Ors., is a positive step taken by ordering the inclusion of the Draft Rules of 2021 in every state, which makes the procedure involved in post-mortem examination a stringent one. The performing of the night post-mortem examination is still not uniform across India. However, there is no need to ban night post-mortems as the lights which are used in the daytime are the same which are used in the night time. With the growth in technology, the bodies even during the daytime are examined inside a room under artificial light, thereby giving no rise to an argument that there is a difference in performing the post-mortem in daytime or night time. Though to perform post-mortems at night, if claimants of the deceased are present, their consent can be taken. Further, the liability of medical officers who conduct post-mortem needs to be regulated as there have been numerous cases wherein such medical officers have tried to turmoil the report or tamper it which in turn affects the trial in court, which is trying to give justice. These are certain observation which has come out from this doctrinal research concerning post-mortem examination in India.

References:

[1] Samuel D. Hodge Jr. & Nicole M. Saitta, Behind Closed Doors of the Coroner's Office - The Medical/Legal Secrets Involving an Autopsy, 32 TEMP. J. Sci. TECH. & ENVTL. L. 1 (2013).

[2] SeventhQueen, *Post-mortem report and it's particulars in forensic science*, Legal Desire (2020), https://legaldesire.com/post-mortem-report-and-its-particulars-in-forensic-science-2/ (last visited Feb 5, 2021).

[3] Susan Ellis Wild, Webster's New World Law Dictionary (2006).

[4] Id.

[5] D. P. Lambert, Some Aspects of Medico-Legal Work in India, 6 MEDICO-LEGAL & CRIMINOLOGICAL REV. 127 (1938).

[6] Samuel D. Hodge Jr. & Nicole M. Saitta, see supra note 1.

[7] Apurba Nandy, *Medicolegal Autopsy and Artefacts in Post-mortem Examination, in* Principles of Forensic Medicine 175–192 (1st ed. 1995).

[8] Id.

[9] Id.

[10] JP Modi, *POST-MORTEM EXAMINATION, in* A Textbook of Medical Jurisprudence and Toxicology 30 (26th ed. 2019).

[11] Id.

[12] Apurba Nandy, see supra note 7.

[13] B. R. Sharma, *Historical and Medico-legal Aspects of Infanticide: An overview*, 46 MED. Sci. & L. 152–156 (2006).

[14] Id.

[15] Samuel D. Hodge Jr. & Nicole M. Saitta, see supra note 1.

[16] Id.

[17] D. P. Lambert, see supra note 5.

[18] O.P. Murty et al., UNIFORM GUIDELINES FOR POST-MORTEM WORK IN INDIA: FACULTY DEVELOPMENT ON STANDARD OPERATIVE PROCEDURES (SOP) IN FORENSIC MEDICINE AND TOXICOLOGY, 30 J. For. Med. Tox. 1–137 (2013).

[19] SeventhQueen, See supra note 2.

[20] JP Modi, see supra note 10.

[21] O.P. Murty, see supra note 18.

[22] JP Modi, see supra note 10.

[23] Id.

[24] Basant Lal Sirohiwal, Luv Sharma & P.K. Paliwal, *Critics and Sceptics of Medico-legal Autopsy Guidelines In Indian Context*, 35 JIAFM 373–377 (2013).

[25] Id.

[26] JP Modi, see supra note 10.

[27] Basant Lal Sirohiwal, Luv Sharma & P.K. Paliwal, see supra note 24.

[28] JP Modi, see supra note 10.

[29] Basant Lal Sirohiwal, Luv Sharma & P.K. Paliwal, see supra note 24.

[30] JP Modi, see supra note 10.

[31] A.I.R. 1972 S.C. 952

[32] MANU/SC/8419/2006

[33] 1999 Cr LJ 3699

[34] MANU/SC/0622/2012

[35] MANU/SC/0292/2021

CHAPTER FIVE

E-GOVERNANCE DURING THE PANDEMIC

Maitreyi Shishir*
**4th Year, BA LLB, Symbiosis Law School, Hyderabad*

Introduction

The growth of technology into various sectors in the world is a well-understood phenomenon. From our smartphones to our air conditioners, from schools to offices, technology has become an indispensable part of all. The twenty-first-generation world cannot imagine living a day without technology. It therefore only makes sense that this change in paradigm would affect one of the most crucial elements of the modern political system- governance. As per UNESCO, the specialized organization of the United Nations, 'governance' means the use of authority, be it political, economic, or administrative, for the smooth management of the nation. 'E- Governance' therefore refers to this performance with the help of electronic mediums, to the general public and agencies, which leads to an easier, quicker, and clearer functioning.

When we look into the social exchange theory, we understand that the participation of a nation is the exchange between the nationals and the State Agency[1]. When such exchange takes place, the nationals participating do not just become gainers (for their personal benefit) causing an upward growth to the private value. Rather, they become a source of the provider of resources. They do so by sharing their personal opinions, actions, etc. which creates public value[2]. E-governance makes and has made this exchange an easier process through its online services.

When the Covid-19 pandemic struck the whole world, there was a sharp boost in the demand and use of e-governance as a tool for convenience and medical safety. Though it was called in in multiple nations, countries specifically like India had a higher demand for the same due to the voluminous population. It was not an easy task to contain almost a population of 1.3 billion people at home without proper services and arrangements by the government. As we are well aware, similar to other countries, to avoid the mass passing of the infection, the whole nation went into a national lockdown.

The initial lockdown was supposed to stay go on from the 25th of March, 2020 to the 14th of April, 2020. This was Phase – 1 of the Lockdown. However, to further prevent the infection, the lockdown was extended to the 3rd of May. This however still continued, as the pandemic showed no sign of control and the limit went on to the 17th of May. Finally, the whole nationwide lockdown extended till the 31st of May. It was only after this that on the 8th of June, the nation started opening up with the Unlock 1.0 and it consistently went on to be relaxed further.[3] These unlocks however were all subjected to certain conditions. Further on, states had their regional lockdowns as well as per the challenges they dealt with. Not everyone was allowed to go out.

But since everyone was locked inside with very little liberty to go out, the government was supposed to provide its people with proper e-governance systems. The Government, therefore, came up with different applications and websites that would make information spreading and information consumption easy. A bright example for the same would be the Arogya Setu app which helped in keeping a track and record of people who were infected, the people who went around them, the total data of the cases and so much more. This application acted as a savior as well as a guide for people to protect themselves and be aware of the number of cases in and around them.

There were many other e-initiatives that were initiated by the government. New administrative mechanisms would include the services of e-Pass for moving outside during the curfew or the online services that was started by the Delhi government to track the availability of beds, oxygen supply etc. for a quick check and easier admission to the hospitals. This paper shall take a look into the system of e-governance, its evolution and its relevance etc. It shall then study the relevance of e-governance during the current pandemic.

Review of Literature

1. E-governance in India: Opportunities and Challenges by *Kiran Yadav and Sanatan Tiwari*[4]

This paper talks about the e-governance system of India. It gives a brief overview of what e-governance is and then immediately moves forward to explain the benefits of e-governance. For the same it provides examples. It then talks about how e-governance is used in various sectors. This is explained very categorically. It then goes on to elaborate on the projects that have taken place under them. This paper was used to understand the relevance of e-governance in India.

2. Dynamics of e-Governance in Post- COVID era by *Upmith Singh, Kamlendra Rawat and Ashima Raj Singhla*[5]

This paper is of analytical nature. It looks into the statistics of the e-governance products that the government has launched during COVID. It also gives us a brief about the evolution of the concept of e-Governance. It then gives an elaborate analysis of the various stats collected. This paper was used to understand the evolution of e-governance and its basic understanding.

3. Second Administrative Reforms Commission Report by *the Government of India*[6]

This report was the eleventh report on e-governance which was made with the view of transforming the governance system in India technologically. It includes within it a detailed understanding of e-governance in the sense of framework and what its scenario exists in India and Internationally. It spoke about the core principles and the national plan for the same. This paper was referred to to understand the footing of e-governance in India.

4. E-governance by *IGNOU*[7]

This document gave an understanding of e-governance. It explained to us the measures that are to be followed before one decides to go for e-governance. It then goes on to explain the work plan and infrastructure for the same. This paper was referred for the general understanding of the e-Governance framework in India.

5. E-Governance: Helping in times of Covid-19 Lockdown by *Jitender Singh and Neha Paliwal*[8]

This paper gives us an insight into the pandemic aspect of e-governance. In the paper, the authors tackle with explaining e-governance and the schemes that were being used during the pandemic. The schemes and their relevance with aspect to the pandemic were understood. This paper was used to understand the relation between the pandemic and the e-governance system.

The Evolution of e-Governance in India

The National Informatics Centre or NIC was established in 1977 when the government understood the value of, and in the advancement of information technology. This was a rare step back then, making it a milestone. To promote the idea of using information technology, the government provided all government offices with computers so that the system could be shifted into one that would be more technologically friendly. However, most of the use was limited to documentation and editing. Companies started using information technology towards generating employee income, creating reports, regulating work and other internal and external functions.

It was in 2006 when the IT initiative was labeled as the 'National e-Governance Plan' or the 'NeGP'. The plan received official approval on the 18th of May. This new initiative brought with it 27 new Mission Mode Projects which looked into bringing in information technology in different areas of governance such as tax recording, banking etc.

We are all aware of the Indian demography and how well-educated people were back then to use technology. This meant that the government had to introduce all these plans from the beginner stage. The government had to pitch these websites as a reliable source and place for the citizens to find information from. Only after they are made aware, the government facilitate this process, making them try the e-portals on their own.

To further technological advancement, the government in 2014 introduced an investment of One Lakh Crore for the development of 'Digital India'. This plan however backfired as the government did not receive sufficient engagements on these platforms as they had perceived. This made the projects fail. Citizens were not keen on using these e-Services to their benefit.[9] Indian citizens were adamant against not using technology in their favour, even if the government was willing to provide them with sufficient investment. How was the government supposed to work in the technology in the system then?

Relevance of e-Governance

E-governance was brought in to revolutionize the government mechanism in a manner that remains up to date with the revolution in the society. The use of technology had boomed and therefore, the government wanted to make sure that this had positive effects even among governance. There were several factors behind why the government pushed the use of technology in governance.

First of all, the usage of e-governance makes the process of governance very quick, easy and cheap in terms of cost of delivery. The entry of technology has made public service very fast-paced. It enables the government to provide citizens with information in a faster manner, with full efficiency and in a manner that is doable for both them and the public. An example for the same would be farmers' ease in accessing the Records of Rights, Tenancy and Crops. Earlier, obtaining the same would take a period of 30 days whereas now, farmers receive the record in 30 minutes. Additionally, the hard copy of this record would require them to pay enough amount of bribe. However, now they can receive it in the meagre amount of 15.

Secondly, e-governance has led to a more accountable government. The amount of transparency that it brings to the system is impeccable. This transparency causes the amount of corruption to decrease. When the internet is so readily available, the citizens become extremely aware of their rights, duties and powers. Since they are aware, the authoritarian powers of government employees are curtailed. Initially, they would take advantage of the lack of knowledge amongst the public. That has drastically reduced. For instance, registering one's land has now become an easy task as the people know what to do leading them to not pay bribe to the officers for the work. The officers are hence not able to harass common men.

Finally, a big achievement the system has brought is the increased levels of participation from the public. As mentioned earlier, the Social Exchange theory talks about the interaction between the State and the Citizens. Since now the people are able to communicate with the government easily, for instance, complaining through the government app. They now have a stronger faith in the government. They become more participative, by adding in their comments and reviews about the government functions. Since they are also aware, the comments or information they provide are of better quality. This makes the process two-way rather than one-way. An example of this would be the recent appeal that the Delhi High Court has made for asking for reviews of people on the Intellectual Property Division Rules. For the same, they provided an email address. This made the process of sending them the review easier and quicker. It definitely increases the amount of participation by the citizens.

The Pandemic Scenario

The mindset of the people, which was against using technology took a 360-degree turn after the Covid – 19 pandemics came leaving us with lockdowns at our dispersal. The importance of e-governance and its services started increasing. The complete lock-in led to creative and innovative technology schemes coming in and creating solutions for the problems that emerged for the governance. As mentioned earlier, one of the biggest tools for the government was the Aarogya Setu app.

This application was brought in by the government. The application uses a combined technology of GPS, Bluetooth, artificial intelligence, and data analytics to bring in qualified data for its users[10]. The application was a lifesaver. People were able to understand the amount of infection around them based on the varying amounts of distances it encompassed. People were also able to know whether they were at risk due to exposure to someone who had Covid. This was done by the constant update on the app with regards to any reported case. People were able to trace back to who was exposed to the virus and whether this person could cause further damage. People were able to regularly test themselves to find out if they had any suspicious symptoms.

Now, the good thing about this app was that it wasn't just good for one side of the party, it was a helpful tool for both. As citizens, we were able to personally make sure we were not exposed to any dangers. The app was used by individuals at their capacity, but also by offices and colleges for any risk assessment. But it was also a powerful tool for the government. They were able to keep a track of the number of people sick, the severity of their case, how many more people could be at risk, etc. This made governance of the pandemic an easier task. But this app was not the only one to jump in. There were many other such initiatives as well.

While the Aarogya Setu app was an initiative of the Central Government, the multiple State governments were also able to partner up with other innovative tech companies to provide better management and governance to their state. The ideas of e-governance that were applied by all the state governments could be segregated into two major ideas: No. 1- Apps for medical and healthcare support and No. 2- state-initiated delivery services.

When we look at the first category segregated, these applications were the ones that were used for the healthcare sector. It majorly dealt with the management of medical facilities. These tools worked using certain aspects of technology. These included a feature for tracking the growth of the infection in the area. They also allowed for the patients and other medical authorities to have an idea of all the infected people and any other data related to it. It then worked as a database to know which hospital has which medical features available in real-time. This also allowed the government to know where they had to supply which medical products.

There are other apps as well that were functioning. These applications played a similar role in knowing about the medical services or products of people around us. They also made it easier for the government as they were also able to receive all the data, such as the bed requirements, oxygen requirements, medicine in deficiency, that allowed them to provide the public with relevant supplies. Their data worked as additional information for the government.

The second category includes other services that are more general in nature but are to be provided by the state. A very popular app under this category is the one that was made to combat providing essentials to those in the containment zone. They also include sending delivery boys to go up and sell their goods on the doorstep to increase the following of the rules of social distancing. Some other apps include those that allowed for slot booking by the customer in stores so that only small groups are present in the market, allowing for a lack of chaos.

The municipal governments also came up with their set of innovations. There were several instances when apps were made that allowed for grocery shop owners to tie up with local street hawkers and cart vendors. They would then ask them, to sell or deliver the goods and ask for the payment via the app so that even they received a certain percentage over the money. The hawkers would then home step deliver the goods and earn a certain amount of money. This way, the government was able to hire people for providing them with household goods.

Now while these tools were made for the government to use for the pandemic, there are also certain other tools that were a creation of the past that received a lot of use during the difficult times. Due to the lack of options, people from government jobs to streets side hawkers, everyone evolved to use the technological achievements of the past. A huge success was brought for online payment. Now, even a flower seller accepts BhimUPI and other payment platforms. This makes it easier for the government to know the amount and size of transactions that are made.

With the pandemic still going on, and with the new world mechanism starting to incorporate the same, the hybrid changes are going to remain for perpetuity. The government has also incorporated the same and shall continue to do so. Not just for the pandemic precautions but also because the State is aware that the use of technology in the governance will lead to a better and more efficient amount of service.

With the pandemic came charges that the government had to face. With the restrictions at work, the nation was faced with a sufficient amount of economic losses. This has led to the government finding various mannerisms to make sure that the economic losses could be reverted back. The state has to make arrangements to make sure that economic activities start taking place and are also supposed to make sure that they are able to provide services to the citizens in a timely and efficient manner. The invasion of technology has helped sufficiently with that.

People can expect continued use of technology along with the current model, also popularly known as the 'Hybrid Mode'. For now, in this short duration, all the initiatives taken by the government towards e-governance were separately made at the Union, State, or Local level. However, time is not far when the center and the state level of the government collab to create integrated e-governance plans, that would have the best practices from both of them. This would bring in more uniformity on the table. It would also lead to a more disciplined yet strong practice by the whole of the government when it comes to services that would be provided by the state. This shall make the use of e-governance more sustainable yet a benefit-boosting opportunity for both the people as well as the government.

Suggestion and Conclusion

E-governance was an unacceptable idea of the past that seems like an essential tool of governance for the present and the future. Today, e-governance acts as a blessing for so many making any problem easy to solve. However, this does not provide us with confirmed confidence. We still do not know whether these behaviors will change back to normal or whether e-Governance has become a revered solution. This makes it necessary for the government to create a strategy to tackle the current scenario while also making sure that the progress in the e-governance system is doing well. Now the government has a stronger footing as not only the technology-friendly people but also those who had no interest in the area had to learn and incorporate their work as per the world of technology. If the strategy that is built is revolutionary and effective, technology can be incorporated easily in the governance of our day-to-day activities.

BIBLIOGRAPHY

References:

1. Arindam Guha. 2020. "Covid-19: Use of New-Age Technologies for e-Governance." *Economic Times Government*. https://government.economictimes.indiatimes.com/news/digital-india/covid-19-use-of-new-age-technologies-for-e-governance/75993744.
2. D Bhattacharya, U Gullu, and M P Gupta. 2012. "E-Service Quality Model for Indian Government Portals: Citizens' Perspective." *Journal of Enterprise Information Management* 25(3): 246–71.
3. "E-Governance." In IGNOU. http://www.ignou.ac.in/upload/B2U2cit-002.pdf.
4. J Alford. 2002. "Defining the Client in the Public Sector: A Social-Exchange Perspective." *Public Administration Review* 62(3): 337–46.
5. J Ju, L Liu, and Y Feng. 2019. "Design of an O2O Citizen Participation Ecosystem for Sustainable Governance." *Information Systems Frontiers* 21(3): 605–20.
6. Jitender Singh and Neha Paliwal. 2020. "E-Governance: Helping in Times of Covid-19 Lockdown." *Journal of Engineering and Technology* 6(2). https://www.gyanvihar.org/journals/index.php/2020/07/23/e-governance-helping-in-times-of-covid-19-lockdown-2/.
7. Kiran Yadav and Sanatan Tiwari. 2014. "E-Governance in India: Opportunities and Challenges." *Advance in Electronic and Electric Engineering* 4(6): 675–80.
8. *Second Admnisitrative Reforms Commission*. 2008. Government of India. https://darpg.gov.in/sites/default/files/promoting_egov11.pdf.
9. Surbhi Gloria Singh. 2020. "Covid-19: Here's a Timeline of Events since Lockdown Was Imposed in India." *BUSINESS STANDARD*. https://www.business-standard.com/article/current-affairs/here-s-a-timeline-of-events-since-lockdown-was-imposed-in-india-120070201413_1.html.
10. Upmith Singh, Kamlendra Rawat, and Ashim Raj Singhla. 2021. "Dynamics of E-Governance in Post COVID Era: India." *The Electronic Journal of Information System in Developing Countries* 87(4).

Citations:

[1] (J Alford, 2002)
[2] (J Ju et al., 2019)
[3] (Surbhi Gloria Singh, 2020)
[4] (Kiran Yadav and Sanatan Tiwari 2014)
[5] (Upmith Singh, Kamlendra Rawat, and Ashim Raj Singhla 2021)
[6] (Second Admnisitrative Reforms Commission 2008)
[7] (E-governance n.d.)
[8] (Jitender Singh and Neha Paliwal 2020)
[9] (D Bhattacharya et al., 2012)
[10] (Arindam Guha 2020)

CHAPTER SIX

INSIDER TRADING – AN INFAMOUS PRACTICE

Apurva Kumar Das*

**Student, Symbiosis Law School,Hyderabad*

INTRODUCTION

The study being conducted with the major purpose being to bring an understanding of what is Insider trading with respect to the stock market. Insider trading can essentially be defined as an Insider (Person occupied and working with knowledge that is sensitive to securities of the said company) who trades the securities or manages deals related to the same before the information is even made available to the general public. It is important to note that a Market tip won't in itself be considered as Insider trading and it is necessary that the person accused can be proved to have in possession status or ways through which access to sensitive information be given. It was initially during the time of the Sachar Committee that company personnel who could influence the market sentiment at the time. To curb the possibility of insider trading a certain time slot was introduced to make sure that the insiders trade during that time. Also the stakeholders who traded would need to have a publication of that information in a certain time frame although mandatorily. Albeit initially the clauses were to be fulfilled on paper ever since the Internet boom the e disclosure system has come into effect. SEBI announced an amendment by strengthening the insider trading rules with clarity in definition and concepts of insider trading. ***Samir C Arora V. SEBI***[1]was observed to be having activities like insider trading fraudulent practices and professional misconduct are detrimental to other traders. This has led to regulation 3 under the SEBI conformed regulations to ban Trading by insiders, this also relays to insider string to be part of or dealing in securities which were part of a sister concern or an associate company. The secondary duty here lies on the hands of the concerned company who have to undertake mandatory measures such as initiating Information received regarding Price sensitive Information and adequate data security of Confidential Information stored on the computer which if not undertaken will result in imposition of penalties that could go up to as much as 25 crores[2] up to as much as thrice the amount in question of being fraudulently transacted. The study shall also include aspects of legal insider trading which as mentioned earlier is allowed under the ambit of being conducted as per the guidelines as prescribed by SEBI, loopholes to the same shall also be bought to light. The current Game stop situation getting so much mainstream attention into the picture also gives us to probably contemplate if the stock market is indeed a market democracy or people at the helm of the market are actually dictating the prices on their own whims and fancies, the biggest economically sound companies got upheaveled due to this[3]. Hence it is rather imperative that the study here shall be largely based on the pros as well as cons of Insider trading and how loopholes if any can be negated so as to reduce the Hinderance by Insider trading to the market at large.

SCOPE

The Scope of the study Entails a need to scrape through the legislatives folds and crevices which have created the possibility of insider trading going unnoticed or rather even possible. The different levels at which Insider can be dne given the range of an Insider from a mere employee to one of the board members or anyone with consequential stake in the company can be detrimental[4]. The scope shall also include the possibility of piercing the corporate veil which could be used to trade money from other associate companies under the same umbrella mixed with personal finances. The scope will also include the affect of such practices in the stock market which shall be inclusive of a study that relates to the effect the outsider's have to face due to any such practices on the inside.

RESEARCH OBJECTIVES

1. To Discover the various Determinants of Insider trading
2. To qualify the abnormal returns to Insider trading strategies'
3. To Decipher the Information Content of Insider trading
4. To try and provide mechanism that can predict the future market conditions due to such offenses

RESEARCH QUESTIONS

1. To ascertain the factors detriment to Insider Trading in India?
2. To Decipher the abnormal returns under Insider trading[5]?
3. To come up with plausible solutions to try and decrease possibility of Insider trading?
4. Can the Prediction for future Market Crashes be predicted through Insider trading?
5. Are the Penalties imposed right now enough to have people think of abstinence from the crime?

LITERATURE REVIEW

- ***Rishikesh Desai and Yosham Desai(2010)*** : The article essentially explains regarding the moral and legal duties those are bestowed upon us as soon as one acquires any kind of insider knowledge before everyone else through a relationship and subsequent consequences arising once the information is wrongly used.
- ***Anil K. Manchikatla and Rajesh H. Acharya(2017)*** **:** the article is about the insiders control over market and being aware of the various threats it proposes the firm involved, UPSI is the key factor in Insider trading and loopholes such as not enough supervision can be detrimental to that.
- ***Adv. Shruti Kakkar, INSIDER TRADING: JOURNEY OF LEGAL FRAMEWORK TO CHECK THE PRACTICE*** : The following paper consisted of statutory evolution of the SEBI regulations in the past fifty years to determine the graph at which the operations have changed s drastically over time and the cases that have shaped the situation over time.
- ***Prerna Chopra, Insider Trading Laws in India*** **:** The following paper could be explained to being a paper based totally on the initial inception of Laws in the country and subsequent addition of other important laws that hinge with the major laws to provide a base to the whole system.
- ***Reema Mali, Insider trading in India – Rules till now*** **:** The paper is an inclusive study of various prevalent rules and parameters that have been set across to curb the practice whilst also at the end incorporating the possible resorts to the current scenario after identifying the Gap.

RESEARCH METHODOLOGY

A number of Quantative as well as Qualitative measures of research have been put to use in order to complete the conducted legal research[6]:

- Formative Legal Research

Formative Research helps researchers identify and understand the intricrices that lay within the disposition of the target population that are certainly influential on the result and decision that can be made. This might hugely affect the developing of programmes undertaken bring across an improvement.

- Doctrinal Research

This form of research Acquaints itself with different Doctrine's of law and other various Propositions. These generally include various cases held on by various courts, this is a common form of research carried on by researchers wherein different judgements are studied and analysed to conclude something regarding the application of such statutes to derive answers in cases and further applied to the ongoing matter that subsists with the court. This is basically relational in nature and works on the general average wherein a certain interpretation that has been accepted at large becomes the standard for reference here.

- Secondary Research

The following method generally entails the study of already collected data that is again study to mould into a certain perspective. Existing data is always condensed again to increase effectiveness of present data for others who might use the data, generally these are used in for the purposes of conducting a sample research or publication somewhere. Many organization's from private to publica are users of such data and generally mine through outsourcing to other entity.

INSIDER TRADING :

The layman explanation to what Insider trading is can be described as the sale or purchase of securities by corporate insiders by virtue of them having insider information just through their position in the firm or the relations they might have at the place. To one's Interest may lay the fact that the contention with regard to Financial Markets when it comes to betting their odds, is it fair that one party has more information than the other but counter culture believes that as such is an intrinsic part of the stock market and hence gathering of Information is totally skill based for anyone participating. However, this is where the Mosaic Theory comes into fruition wherein it is understood that any public information interpreted for benefit cannot be undertaken as being unfair while dealing in the stock exchange and thus obtaining any sort of private information that might be detrimental to the performance of the stock in a given scenario is something that is to be considered. This is off course information that is to be deemed detrimental in nature only when the information is of nature that could probably cause a fluctuation in the markets.

There is new word that is included under the new amended act which is 'Original Information' given in ***section 7A(h)*** of the latest act. Original Information means any independent Knowledge or information which is not known board which isn't frivolous. Insiders have found that insider trading has manipulated the prices of the stock market multiple times leading to major strains on the economy as whole or at least sectorally. There have been few efforts but sparsely enough in the past couple of decades but a sole insurance of non revelation of identity of the person who bust's such a scam, doesn't turn out to be the most lucrative offer for many, While scamsters such as Harshad Mehta were caught doing the same, their tales have been glorified to getting the people believe that it was harmless and cunning on his end of the spectrum[7].

IndiaBulls Insider Trading Case

This case is the latest law which is related to insider trading[8], India bulls was severely accused on to an amount of 87 Lakhs for a couple of their employees garnered insider information and traded on the same to make a sole profit which clearly falls under the ambit of unfair Insider trading here in India[9]. The people involved were a part of the top tier management of the company and hence were seen to be involved in other unlawful gains as well upon research, this led to action against them by the IVF and penalty as well as punishment were duly imposed.

The main aim in such an effort is with relation to Insider efforts and "Unpublished information". Insiders trading Laws encourage the distribution of securities in stringent countries.

SEBI AND IT'S ROLE

SEBI is the paragon of banking institution in India, it is considered to being the authoritative body that exists in India which looks over the regulation as well as development of their banking Entities in the country. SEBI in the same breath hence is also largely responsible towards overlooking the various aspects of Investors as well as securities. Insider trading in India is an offense for which a penalty as well as imprisonment could be levied. While this can be studied as being a Mixture of Civil as well as Criminal laws, certainly it isn't as stringent as probably one requires a law to be to serve the purpose of keeping such criminals and defaulters at bay. One of the cases highlighting the vulnerability of the SEBI's in situations concerning Insider trading could be observed to be the ***Rakesh Aggarwal v. SEBI*[10]**, In the following case, Mr. Aggarwal who was the Managing Director of ABS industries ltd. was concerned with Bayer A.G. for dealing negotiations that related to the possibility of ABS being taken over by Bayer A.G. and this resulted in him having secretive information that was unpublished yet at his disposal. Upon his wrong doings concerning Insider trading he was fined over the amount already unfairly siphoned off with statue section 15(g) being imposed to run proceedings were issued as was the application of 24 of the SEBI act.

A similar Precedent from the case of ***Samir C.Arora v. SEBI***[11]could be established wherein an imposition of a restriction was duly observed which was close to five years on being even allowed to participate in the stock market.

While these are some of the rather highlighted cases currently available as of this moment in the country, Infosys Technologies Ltd was quite definitely the first company to have been the result of an Insider trading check. The penalties and scrutinization of both accused namely Jeffery Lehman as well as Mr. Gopalkrishna, This opened wyes of many people towards Section 195 of the Company Act,2013 along with sections 12A, 15G[12] of the securities and Exchange Board of India Act,1992.

While as discussed above regarding the implications with civil as well as Criminal statutes comparatively not able to satisfy the situation, SEBI could potentially try something similar as a resort for such cases as tried in the Steve Madden case over in the state's[13]. This means a page could be taken out of the book of the case wherein upon the revelation that Madden was guilty of insider trading with his own company, not only was a penalty being imposed on him but also there was an imposition of an amount that was calculated to have been lost by investors, it was calculated considering the factors such as trade, bets made on a stock and how it might have earned investors[14].

To gain an elaborate understanding of insider Trading. I strongly believe one can delve int area of intrigue such as the journey of the laws that we have today for insider trading, from their inception to their subsequent inception :

A. ***Sachar Committee(1979)*[15]** : The high powered Expert Committee on companies and Monopolies and Restrictive Trade Practices Act(MRTP) was constituted in June 1977 for reviewing the companies act. The two major recommendation's that were established by the Sacchar Committee Report were with regards to the full disclosure of people who know about the sensitive Information and more importantly than to devise timelines wherein certain people would be disallowed to engage in trading activities for a given amount of time.
B. ***Patel committee(1987)*[16] :** Whilst the Sacchar Committee report was based on finding solution to the issue at hand, This time around the focus majorly shifted around and about the how such crimes are being facilitated. In It's report it had been found that insider trading is rampant in stock exchanges in the country how internal parameters might be required to set in order to fulfil that scenario.
C. ***Abid Hussain Committee(1989)*** – The working group was essentially formulated to make sure that fresh offenses that could tie down Civil and criminal proceedings. It dealt with efforts to insure that transactions costa are not increased for Investors and rather the correct price is sought.

While as indicated above we surely can observe that India has tried it's fair share of approaches to try and curtail the practice of insider trading, A valid effort could maybe put through by taking Inspiration from something that is being implemented in the states quite successfully, the ***MISAPPROPRIATION*** theory[17]. This act also requires all directors, Officers and beneficial owners to give in their written consent/statement regarding which stock market to list the stock on. While this could be seen as an effort to maintain transparency, in July of 2020, a few amendments were Introduced to the Prohibition of Insider Trading Regulations,2020, to introduce further changes to the PIT regulations, which can be summarized to being the following :

- Introduction for additional transactional mechanisms which can be an alternative or treated as an exception to Window restrictions.

Prior to the PIT Amendment, the board of directors of a listed company were required to be simply maintaining a structured list. SEBI recently also mandated the onus on the company to make sure that the UPSI has been shared with the Intermediaries/fiduciaries, the listed company would be required to maintain details of the recipient entity, which in turn would make sure that everything listed on the database will have a digital receipt.

- Enhancement of the Structured Digital Database towards seeking and storing additional details of persons sharing unpublished information. Similarly with the new extension of rules with regards to punishing the offenders, The PIT Amendment doesn't clarify the mechanism for such intimation, the payment details rather any sort of transactive details are going to be published exclusively.
- The reporting authority was also changed which led to automation procedures for disclosures of PIT Violations by listed entities. Along with which the SEBI would also now be required to be kept in loop with the punishments being meted out to the defaulters as well as transparency regarding the misappropriated amount.

HINDUSTAN LIVER LIMITED V. SEBI

The case revolves around the involvement of HLL and their undertaking of Brooke Bond Lipton India limited, While SEBI found out that, at time of the purchase of shares HLL was considered an Insider as can be highlighted by section 2(e) of the 1992 regulations, which are as follows:

"(i) is or was connected with the company or is deemed to have been connected with the company and is reasonably expected to have access by virtue of such connection to unpublished price sensitive information in respect of securities of the company, or

(ii) has received or has had access to such unpublished price sensitive information."

The issue was created as the purchase was made a mere two weeks before the evitable merger of HLL with BBLIL. It was also published verifiably that the company already knew about the Merger and which according to SEBI is enough evidence to understand that there was a Lapse in fair play here. The appellate authority agreed with the SEBI, HLL could be potentially be termed as an issue as both were under the same parent company.

A set of dual agreements were put forward by the Appellate authority with contentions of HLL that, for the information to be considered as UPSI, the following couple of guidelines were required to be mandatorily followed:

1. ***"The information must not be <u>generally known</u> or published by the company; and***
2. ***If published or known, is likely to materially affect the prices of securities of that company in the market."***

Subsequently a Contention was observed from the Appellate authority wherein the evidence produced by HLL cannot be classified as UPSI as the information's regards to their merger was public information, posted right through newspapers to online blogs to listicles.

There were also contentions made in the light of the arguments that the information of the merger in no way would actually affect the price of the companies stock and hence this is a conversation that shouldn't be actually taking place. However, the authorities believe that just the scale of the entities involved is too huge right now to consider that argument.

SEBI referred to the 2015 regulations, wherein they had mentioned about the Internal code of conduct:

- ***"Unless a promoter is designated as a "Designated Person" by the Board of Directors in consultation with their compliance officer, no pre-clearance for trading is needed.***
- ***There exists an assumption that the actions of compliance officers, Board of Directors and other entities entrusted with ensuring adherence to Insider Trading Regulations, should be to ensure compliance with the regulatory framework and not for an "ulterior motive".***
- ***An action of a compliance officer, whether it is extraneous to his or her powers, is to be examined by the Board of Directors and the audit committee.***
- ***The 2015 Regulations by nature are prohibitive and the applicability of its provisions is with respect to insiders and such concerned securities to which a UPSI might pertain. This is to avoid any undue advantage accrued to classes of investors on account of their access to UPSI."***

CONCLUSION

As seen through the course of the paper, there are a number of different laws which supplement the basic law which qualifies the act of Insider trading to be an offense. SEBI, acting as the paragon body to all banks has the onus of looking after the various parties involved, from looking after that the investor are safe to making sure there is fair play in the market by virtue of having a clear demarcation regarding what is Illegal insider trading and what is Legal Insider Trading. While there is an unfortunate realisation regarding how the situation can never be made fool proof, yet there is certainly a requirement of a scenario that makes sure that there is no lapse of parameters by trying to bring in measures that are strict and applicable to a companies inner workings. There could be certain possibilities such as undertaking measure's which ensure that there is maintenance of secerey for a particular time frame wherein the company is going for an IPO. Also the penalties that are currently applicable need to be reworked so as to make sure that there is a fear for anyone who wishes to indulge in such an activity.

BIBLIOGRAPHY

SOURCES

- Definition of Insider Trading,Economictimes,22 April 2021,12:36 PM IST, https://economictimes.indiatimes.com/definition/insider-trading
- Abumustafa, N.I. and Nusair, S.A. (2011). "Insider trading during the 2008 financial crisis." Applied Financial Economics, 21(5), 301-307.
- Satvik Varma, "Is India too soft on insider traders?" https://economictimes.indiatimes.com/slideshows/economy/is-india-too-soft-on-insider-traders/insider-tradingis-a-criminal-offence/slideshow/11066581.cms
- Himanshu Chahar, Insider Trading in India, http://www.legalserviceindia.com/article/l199-InsiderTrading.html (last visited Feb 28, 2019)
- Dutta, S. and Nitani, M. (2008). "Corporate governance and informed trading." International Journal of Managerial Finance, 4(4), 295-322. Jaffe, J.F. (1974). "Special information and insider trading." The Journal of Bus

STATUTES

1. Securities and Exchange Board of India Act,1992.
2. Companies Act , 2013
3. Insider Trading Regulations,2020
4. The Bombay Securities Contracts Control Act, 1925
5. The SEBI Act, 1992

REPORTS

1. Sachar Committee Recommendations, No-18.104 (iv)
2. Patel Committee Recommendations, No-7.26

CASES

1. Rakesh Aggarwal v. SEBI ,(2004) 1 CompLJ 193 SAT, 2004 49 SCL 351 SAT
2. Samir C.Arora v. SEBI ,[2005] 59 SCL 96 (SAT-Mum)
3. INDIABULL'S CASE

Citations:

[1] [2005] 59 SCL 96 (SAT)

[2] The Bombay Securities Contracts Control Act, 1925

[3] The SEBI Act, 1992

[4] Abumustafa, N.I. and Nusair, S.A. (2011). "Insider trading during the 2008 financial crisis." Applied Financial Economics, 21(5), 301-307.

[5] Dutta, S. and Nitani, M. (2008). "Corporate governance and informed trading." International Journal of Managerial Finance, 4(4), 295-322. Jaffe, J.F. (1974). "Special information and insider trading." The Journal of Bus

[6] . *Legal Education and Research Methodology* by Dr. Mono Purohit, *Central Law Publication*

[7] Definition of Insider Trading,Economictimes,22 April 2021,12:36 PM IST, https://economictimes.indiatimes.com/definition/insider-trading

[8] Indiabulls Securities limited v. Securities and Exchange Board of India, www.sebi.gov.in/satorders/indiabulls

[9] Companies Act,2013,Section 11(2)E of Companies Act

[10] (2004) 1 CompLJ 193 SAT, 2004 49 SCL 351 SAT

[11] [2005] 59 SCL 96 (SAT-Mum)

[12] 15(G) of the securities and Exchange Board of India Act,1992.

[13] Himanshu Chahar, Insider Trading in India, http://www.legalserviceindia.com/article/l199-InsiderTrading.html (last visited Feb 28, 2019)

[14] Satvik Varma, "Is India too soft on insider traders?" https://economictimes.indiatimes.com/slideshows/economy/is-india-too-soft-on-insider-traders/insider-tradingis-a-criminal-offence/slideshow/11066581.cms

[15] Sachar Committee Recommendations, No-18.104 (iv)

[16] Patel Committee Recommendations, No-7.26

[17] 2 Seyhun Nejat H. (1998), " Investment Intelligence from Insider Trading" , The MIT Press,

CHAPTER SEVEN

Auditor: Rights, Duties, and Liabilities

Maitreyi Shishir*

**4th Year, BA LLB, Symbiosis Law School, Hyderabad*

Introduction

Every company functions on funds given by someone else. This person does not interfere or take part in the daily activities of the company. However, as the provider of the capital utilized by the company on a day-to-day purpose, they would like to make sure that all the money is utilized effectively. They would want to make sure that the company represents the utilization of the money in the right manner in the various records of the company including the annual records.

For this function to take place, there is a requirement of an individual who has no obligation or liability with the company and who works independently and is employed outside of the company. His main task is to review and inspect the accounts of the company in a timely manner. He has to, in an efficient and honest manner, make sure that there exists no fraud in the company's financial records, and that there is no error whatsoever. This person is the auditor.

The task of an auditor is to look into the finance-related aspect of the company from a third-party view. The non–relation of the auditor with the company with its own rights and duties that are kept in check with its liabilities allows for the healthy functioning of the company. He works with the company, receives his remuneration from them as well, but does not provide its services to them. The statute allows for certain prohibitions which makes sure that even though he works at the company, he remains independent and does not serve their interests.[1] The auditor, therefore, works as an agent and an officer of the company.

The main motive behind bringing in the procedure of auditing in the company is to make sure that the company represents all its profits, losses and all other financial data accurately to the government, the investors, the subscribers and the public in general. There has been an alarming rise in the cases of fraud done by companies. The procedure of auditing reduces such chances by large margins by looking into any mistakes or frauds from the very initiation of the company.

The minimum requirement for a person to be an auditor is to be qualified as a Chartered Accountant. This requirement is mandatory. The provisions of the act also allow for a firm to be appointed as an auditor, except that only those members with a valid Chartered Accountant certification shall be allowed to act as one.

Research Methodology

This research shall be based on Doctrinal Legal Research Methodology. The research shall focus on studying the "Indian Companies Act of 2013" and its various sections to understand the rights, duties and liabilities of an Auditor of a company. Secondary Sources of data like Books, Research Papers and Journal Articles shall also be used with the help of Jstor and other databases.

Chapterisation

1. Introduction

This chapter shall make us familiar with who is an auditor, why is he appointed, what is the objective of the auditing process and who can be appointed as an auditor.

2. Rights of an Auditor

This chapter shall enlist and explain the various rights that are available to an Auditor for his independent functioning.

3. Duties of an Auditor

This chapter shall enlist and explain the duties that are expected of an auditor to make sure that the company functions correctly.

4. Liabilities of an Auditor

This chapter shall enlist and explain the liabilities that can arise if the auditor does not follow his duties correctly.

5. Judicial Decisions

This chapter shall look into various landmark judgments with regards to auditors in both the Indian and the English Courts

6. Conclusion

This chapter shall wrap up and conclude the topic.

Rights of an Auditor

The successful discharge of the duties of an auditor is very important. That is why the lawmakers have ensured that the auditors receive enough rights to discharge their duty. These rights that have been provided, therefore, are statutory in nature. This makes it impossible for any Article or Memorandum to abridge, infringe or confine their scope. The courts have in fact reiterated it several times as well[2]. The rights of an auditor are mentioned below:

Right to access the books and accounts

As per the provisions of sub-clause (1)[3] allows for all and any auditor to access the company's books, accounts and vouchers at any time. The time duration however of 'at any times' limits itself to only the business hours that are normally followed. A voucher includes any such document that deals with any information of the transactions or the information that is present in the financial statement, in both direct and indirect manner. An example of the same would be an agreement. Books include both the statistical and fiscal books. If the company is a holding company, in that case the auditor also has control over the records of all its subsidiary and associate companies. This requirement includes the prerequisite that the records should be in relation to the consolidation of the financial statement between the two company types.[4]

Right to information and explanation

Section 143 (1) also allows for the auditors to gain access to any information through the officers assigned to the company. They can demand any information and explanation as long as it helps them in performing their duties. Along with that, the auditor has the right to specifically ask about the below–mentioned topics:

- The debts and advances that have been taken by the company stating it to be a security are secured in the right manner and that the conditions it has been based on are not detrimental to the members of the company or the company in general.
- Transactions entered into by the company that is mentioned simply through book entries are not detrimental to the company and its interests.
- The shares, debentures and other securities of the company, that form part of the assets, are not sold at a rate lower than the rate the company purchased it in, in cases where the company is not an investment or banking company.
- Deposits of the company display the loans and advances made by the company.
- Revenue account is utilized for the purpose of personal expenditures.

Right to audit account of a Branch

Branch offices[5] are also a part of the company. As their part, they also need to be audited. Therefore, the companies act provides for the auditing of a branch office to be done by an auditor or any other person who is qualified enough to be an auditor[6]. In case of the branch office being located in a foreign region, the office is supposed to be audited by an auditor, an accountant or any other person who is qualified enough to be an auditor as per the laws of this foreign region the branch office is situated in. However, when the auditing procedure is executed by a person who is not designated as the auditor, he shall submit a record to the officially designated auditor.[7]

Right to certify a report

Every auditor has the right to certify or sign over any report or documents of the company as and when required[8]. In case if a firm or Limited Liability Partnership is designated in the position of an auditor, then only the chartered accountants of the firm can be given the authority to certify or sign over the documents of the company in place of the firm[9]. This means that no partner of the firm or LLP can be given the authority to sign or certify the documents if he is not a chartered accountant.

Right to obtain any notice

It is the right of the auditor to receive any and all notice of any other communication made between all the members with regards to the general meeting of the company[10]. All such communications shall be redirected to the auditor to make a note.

Right to be present at the General Meeting

Every auditor has the right to be present in every general meeting. He also has the right to put his opinion on the table. This right is with regards to any aspect of the meeting that deals with his position as the auditor[11]. He can pitch in his opinions, statements and explanation whenever he feels is necessary for the accounts. If he feels so, he may also send in any of his representatives if he cannot attend the meeting or if he feels it necessary to. It is also necessary that if any of the reports made by the auditor, or any transaction matters that are recorded, may be detrimental to the company's reputation, the members of the company may read it and may inspect it if needed.

Right to salary and indemnification

Every auditor has the right to receive the salary for the services he has provided for the work he has completed. He also has the right to receive indemnification for any blame on him that may take place against him by the company for any civil or criminal proceedings.

Right to assistance

The auditor has the right to take any help from necessary experts with regard to law or technicalities if he finds it necessary.

Duties of an Auditor

Every freedom comes with its responsibilities; every right comes with a duty. The duties of an Auditor serve as no exception. We are all aware generally that an auditor's day-to-day duties is reserved for dealing with the financial aspects of the company. However, there are certain duties that are mandatorily mentioned in the act. These are:

Duty to report the Financial Statements

The first and most prominent duty of the auditor is to make a report on all the financial statements that are presented before the general meeting and with regard to all the accounts that he has examined[12]. The auditor has to make sure that his report represents all the financial transactions of the company to the best of his knowledge and awareness. The report should signify the company's position throughout the financial year and should represent the profit and losses incurred to the company at the end of the financial year accurately. However, this duty is restricted to the auditor's understanding after taking reasonable care and precaution. The auditor is not liable to take the guarantee that no error has taken place at all.

The report shall look into all the financial details. It shall answer questions such as whether the company has provided for a proper book of accounts as instructed by the law, whether the balance sheet gives an accurate representation of all the gains and losses incurred by the company, the auditor's analysis on the financial undertakings, whether a proper check has been made on the records maintained and more.

Duty to be present at General meeting

The right to state his opinions in the general meeting comes with its compulsion to attend the general meetings of the company[13]. The auditor can attend the meeting in person or appoint a representative to join. This representative, however, should be someone who is qualified to be an auditor as per the Indian laws.

Duty to disclose any fraud

It is the duty of the Auditor to make sure that if there are any discrepancies leading to fraud, he should immediately report it to the Central Government. He may do so if he is of the belief that the company has caused or is facing the commission of fraud through or by the employees or members of the company that can be amounted to rupees one crore or more[14]. For reporting such fraudulent acts, a report needs to be forwarded by the auditor to the audit committee of the company or the Board within 2 days from finding such information out. The time provided for a reply should be forty-five days. After receiving the response from them, the auditor has to send his response or observation to the response to the center within a fortnight.

Duty to make reports for a prospectus

The duties of an auditor also include him making a report for the profits and loss of the company. Such a report shall be attached to the prospectus of the company. The report shall include the gains and losses of the last five financial years preceding the matter and the assets and liabilities of the company which shall include the information until the last date of when such report was made for the prospectus.

Duty to follow the Articles

It is the duty of the Auditor to be aware of all the rules and regulations under the Articles and Memorandum of Association. It is also his duty to make sure that he follows these articles and memorandums as prescribed.

Duty to present evidence

It is the duty of the auditor to keep with him and present when required all the records and financial documents of the company. He may do so in case he is required to present the same to an inspector or any other person he has appointed for the same with the prior permission of the Central Government. He is supposed to assist this inspector or appointed person with any help that he may require, that is available to the auditor in his reasonable capacity, for investigating the case.

Duty to follow their duty

This duty has arisen after various judgments that have been given by the judiciary. It is a well-established fact that the auditors are supposed to take all the necessary steps required to follow all their duties that are prescribed under the act[15]. However, there is a new stand by the government that the people have to take all the necessary steps to follow any additional duty that may be assigned to them through the articles of the company. They cannot give any excuse in the court of law that they were not statutorily bound to follow the prescribed duties.[16]

Duty to certify the report

Every auditor has the duty, to its counterpart right, to certify or sign over any report or documents of the company as and when required[17]. In case a firm or Limited Liability Partnership is designated in the position of an auditor, then only the chartered accountants of the firm shall have the authority to certify or sign over the documents of the company in place of the firm[18]. This means that no partner of the firm or LLP shall be expected to be the authority to sign or certify the documents if he is not a chartered accountant.

Liabilities of an Auditor

Every power and duty brings with it a liability. The auditor also has some liabilities in case he makes an error. These liabilities include:

Liability to negligence

It is the duty of the auditor to look into all the financial transactions and documents. Such inquiry that he takes should have some minimum standards and should be practiced with reasonable care and skills. Therefore, if there are any mistakes in the reports, that bring damages to the company, and that is a mistake that was caused by the mere negligence of the auditor, he shall be held liable for all such damages. It shall be his duty to indemnify the company of the damages caused by his recklessness.

Liability to known mistakes

If any auditor states a false statement on a material topic knowingly, knowing that it can cause damages, or if he omits any facts, or if he represents any false information in the prospectus with knowledge of it being false, he shall be held liable to pay the damages, the refund, the fine as well as serve imprisonment. This does not mean that the reports of an auditor should be out of errors. It only signifies that the auditor has to inspect the report to the best of his capabilities. If the auditor has completed the auditing process in a competent manner acceptable to his professional caliber, he shall not be held liable for any errors in the report.

Liability through breach of trust

If any company has reached to the point of winding up, and in the due procedure of winding up it has been recognized that the auditor has caused a breach of trust to the company, then in those cases, he can be made liable as an officer of the company. In such cases, the court can look into the matter and decided upon a sum of money that the auditor shall have to provide as compensation to the breach of trust they have done to the assets of the company

Liability for an untrue prospectus

In case the auditor makes false claims in the prospectus of the company while inviting for new subscribers of debentures and shares, he as an expert, shall be liable to indemnify each and every subscriber who subscribed to the shares and debentures based on the profit and loss figures that were represented by him.

Liability to not cease through agreement

If there is an agreement made between the company and the auditor, that in case of any specific liability arising, the auditor shall not be liable, all such agreements are considered void by the law. This means that no agreement can free the auditor of any of his liabilities.

Criminal Liability under IPC

If the auditor signs or certifies any such document, that he is aware from his own knowledge is false or wrong, he shall be punishable in the equivalent of a person who furnishes false evidence to the law.[19]

Judicial Decisions

There are few judgments that have been made with regard to auditors over the years.

"Dhrangadhra Chemical Works v. State of Saurashtra[20]"

The Supreme Court held in the case that a Chartered Accountant, who serves as a full-time employee, or who works under the control or supervision of the company, cannot be appointed as the auditor for the same. This decision was based on the basic principle that if the auditor is an employee of the company, he shall not work in an unbiased manner and shall therefore try to cover up or overlook the mistakes or defaults that have been made by the company in its financial transaction. To explain what control by the company meant, the court stated that the extent of control a company had over its employees is very subjective. Therefore, one needs to look into each individual in a subjective manner and understand whether the company holds any control over them or supervises them in executing their job.

"Newton v. Birmingham Small Arms Co.[21]"

This case deals with the rights that are available to an auditor. The English courts stated that no rights that are provided to an auditor through a statute can be limited or infringed by the means of creating newer rights in the company's articles. The rights of an auditor are statutory and are made so to make sure that they have a secured position in the company. These rights enable the auditor to execute all his responsibilities in an independent and fair manner. These rights enable them to work independently and present any mistakes, frauds or wrongdoings that the company is committing.

"London and Genral Bank Ltd. [22]

This case dealt with the extent of an auditor's accuracy while dealing with making reports. It was stated that every auditor is only expected to execute his duties under reasonable care and skills. He does not have an absolute liability over any mistakes that may occur. He is only expected to carry on his duties to the best of his capabilities and as per industry standards.

"Council of the Institute of Chartered Accountants of India v. B. Ram Goel[23]"

The case held that the main objective behind an auditor looking into the financial transactions of the company is to make sure that the company represents its finances in the most accurate and right manner. The act of finding out any fraud or mistake is not the main objective but is something that is achieved while going through the same. If he believes that such fraud or mistake is detrimental, then he can take it into consideration.

"Re Bolivie Expolration Syndicate[24]

The court stated that auditors have to take all the necessary steps to follow any additional duty that may be assigned to them through the articles of the company. Their duties are not just limited to the ones stated under the act. If they fail at performing any duty that is levied on them by the company's articles, they cannot give any excuse in the court of law that they were not statutorily bound to follow the duties

Conclusion

The authority of an auditor has increasingly started to grow and assert importance in the world of corporate governance. With the sudden increase in the number of frauds by companies taking place, the role of an auditor in finding out any irregularity in the initial steps has become essential. Their holistic mechanism in making sure that all the financial transactions and documents are well put helps in a healthy functioning of the company and in return, the economy. With this growing importance, there has been a growth in the independence of the auditor with the help of statutorily defined duties and rights while being held liable too.

References:

[1] The Companies Act, 2013, § 141 (3) and § 144, No. 18, Acts of Parliament, 2013 (India)
[2] Newton v. Birmingham Small Arms Co., (1906) 2 Ch 37
[3] The Companies Act, 2013, § 143 (1), No. 18, Acts of Parliament, 2013 (India)
[4] The Companies Act, 2013, Provisio to § 143 (1), No. 18, Acts of Parliament, 2013 (India)
[5] The Companies Act, 2013, § 2 (14), No. 18, Acts of Parliament, 2013 (India)
[6] The Companies Act, 2013, § 143 (8), No. 18, Acts of Parliament, 2013 (India)
[7] The Companies (Audit and Accounts) Rules, 2014, Rule 12, (India)
[8] The Companies Act, 2013, § 145, No. 18, Acts of Parliament, 2013 (India)
[9] The Companies Act, 2013, § 141 (20), No. 18, Acts of Parliament, 2013 (India)
[10] The Companies Act, 2013, § 146, No. 18, Acts of Parliament, 2013 (India)
[11] The Companies Act, 2013, § 146, No. 18, Acts of Parliament, 2013 (India)
[12] The Companies Act, 2013, § 143 (2) and (5), No. 18, Acts of Parliament, 2013 (India)
[13] The Companies Act, 2013, § 140, No. 18, Acts of Parliament, 2013 (India)
[14] The Companies Act, 2013, § 143 (12), No. 18, Acts of Parliament, 2013 (India)
[15] Re Bolivie Exploration Syndicate, [1913] 3 TLR 146
[16] Leeds Estate Building Investment Co. V. Shephard, [1887] 36 Ch
[17] The Companies Act, 2013, § 145, No. 18, Acts of Parliament, 2013 (India)
[18] The Companies Act, 2013, § 141 (20), No. 18, Acts of Parliament, 2013 (India)
[19] The Indian Penal Code, 1860, § 197, No. 45, Acts of Parliament, 1860 (India)
[20] Dhrangadhra Chemcical Works v. State of Saurashtra, AIR 1957 SC 264
[21] Newton v. Birmingham Small Arms Co. [1906]2 Ch. 37
[22] London and General Bank Ltd., (1895) 2 Ch 673
[23] Council of the Institute of Chartered Accountants of India v. B. Ram Goel[2001] 29 SCL 257
[24] Re Bolivie Exploration Syndicate, [1913]3 TLR 146

CHAPTER EIGHT

CRITICAL ANALYSIS ON ABORTION LAWS

Amrit Raj*

**Student of Symbiosis Law School, Noida.*

Introduction –

Despite several amendments made by legislation, still Women are left back to avail their fundamental rights and also, they do not only face lack of safe abortion but also lack of reproductive rights. Now, et us discuss the meaning of word 'abortion'. The word abortion means cease the exist of pregnancy by way of induced procedure only when the foetus has not grown to the extent to sustain on its own i.e., termination of an infant who yet does not have life in it. The Abortion laws in India started after passing of the *Indian Penal Code, 1860. Section 312*[1]talks about abortion laws which states that "*criminalises forceful abortion and further describe it as miscarriage caused intentionally.*"

Types of Abortion: -

The Abortion can be of two types i.e., Spontaneous abortion and Induced abortion. Spontaneous abortion means abortion done automatically without any external pressure. It is also known as miscarriage and can occur due to many reasons like any trauma or hypertension related to any past event leading to lots of pressure and further miscarriage. Out of total number of pregnancies, around 20 – 30 % of abortion takes place through this Spontaneous Abortion.

Whereas, talking about Induced Abortion, it takes place with the help of external force to get the abortion done. In easier terms it can be explained as abortion done intentionally by using some external force.

When talking about abortion, a majority of population takes this term under Induced Abortion only. Induced Abortion is also considered as a safe step for termination if done appropriately. On the other hand, talking about Unsafe Abortion as per termed by WHO (World Health Organisation), it is a "*process of getting a termination of pregnancy done by any individual who does not have necessary training or termination done in an environment which is not even comfortable for a minimal medical standard.*"[2] Out of total pregnancies, 50 million abortion are done every year out of which around 40% of abortion are done hazardously.

But with the time, the rate of abortion is decreasing and also majority of abortion are done in a safe and appropriate mode because of many acts and also public awareness.

Ways to get an Abortion done: -

During Ancient times, abortion was done in an unsecure manner by way of some natural medication i.e., plants based or through some sharp object or forceful massage and even many more. But now, science has developed a lot and so the termination of pregnancy can be done in much more secured form like through surgeries done by the help of Manual Vacuum Aspiration (MVA) in which the foetus is removed from placenta and membrane of the body by the process of suction done with suction – pump. Another way through which termination of pregnancy can be done is through Dilation & Evacuation Method (D&E). Under this process, the Uterus is removed from the body by operating it and further with the process of suction it is taken out.

Another method is medical abortions. This method of abortion was introduced by *Abortification Pharmaceuticals.* Under this method the termination is done through medicine. As per "*Cochrane Systematic Review 2020, providing women with medications to take home to complete the second stage of procedure for an early medical abortion resulted in effective and health abortion"*[3]

Consequences of such termination –

With such methods of abortion, it can affect someone either physically or mentally.

Physically: -

- It can cause problems like continuous vomiting, abdominal pain and diarrhoea.
- It can also cause infection inside the body and can damage parts of body.
- It can also stop further pregnancies and can also lead to death if not done in a proper manner.

Mentally: -

- It can cause stress and can deteriorate the mental health.
- It can also cause sexual disfunction and can further lead to relationships problem.
- It can lead to depression.

Abortion Laws in India –

Before 1971, termination of pregnancy was considered as unlawful and was criminalised under *Section 312 – 316[4] of the Indian Penal Code, 1860 (IPC)* only in cases where abortion was done for causing miscarriage are punished with imprisonment for 3 years or fine or both, and in case of Woman, the custody period increases to 7 years. The only exception to it is in cases where the termination takes place to save the life of women. Further, after when the abortion became legal in India, abortion rate along with maternal mortality rate started to increase. With this the government of India connected with Shah committee in the year 1964 which was led by Shantilal Shah.

The Shah Committee expanded the legal and medical aspects of abortion law. The committee suggested to permit termination as it will stop wastage of woman's life and health. Further, the recommendations given by Shah Community were appreciated and were presented before the Parliament in the year 1970. This led to passing of a bill i.e., *Medical Termination of Pregnancy (MTP) Bill.* The bill was passed by the parliament in the very next year in August, 1971 which led to the formation of act i.e., *Medical Termination of Pregnancy Act, 1971 (MTP Act).*

Medical Termination of Pregnancy Act -

After the abortion was legalised in India, Medical Termination of Pregnancy Act came into force in the year 1971. It allowed termination of pregnancy till 20 weeks of pregnancy. The Act allowed abortion only in ce1rtain conditions that are :-

- If there is a threat to life of pregnant women.
- If it is assumed that the baby if born might face some serious consequences like he remains disable due to some bodily abnormalities. Although it should be done within 20 weeks of pregnancy and under consultation of two doctors.
- If the pregnancy took place due to rape the termination can take place so that it does not affect the mental health of the girl.

Who can terminate a pregnancy -

The termination of pregnancy can be done by a "***registered medical practitioner***" who has the knowledge in the field of gynaecology as per the *MTP Act* and also has a proper medical qualification mentioned under *Indian Medical Council Act[5] (IMC Act).*

Further due to many problems in the act, it was amended in the year 2020 which led to the enforcement of "*Medical Termination of Pregnancy (Amendment) Act, 2021*"[6] last year on 24 September by the approval of the Union Cabinet. The Act modifies the "*Medical Termination of Pregnancy Act, 1971*"[7] also known as the *"MTP Act"*, which relates to pregnancy termination. The amending Act aims to modify *Section 3[8]*the Act thereby increasing the upper limit of pregnancy termination to 24 weeks, from 20-weeks, for certain categories of women. The rules have now made it easy for women to stop an unwanted pregnancy contrary to the earlier procedure where women had to go through a lengthy process to end up their pregnancy after 20 weeks which further violated Women's Reproductive Rights.

Background of MTP Act in India –

The abortion law in India comes under *Section 312-316[9]*of the *"Indian Penal Code (IPC)"* and under the *MTP Act, 1971[10]*. The *MTP Act, 1971* is one of an exception to *"voluntarily causing a woman to miscarry"* and this further leads to punishment of up to 3 years.[11] It is pertinent to note that the legislations do not set up a rights-based framework or decriminalize abortion. It is the medical practitioners' legislation that aims to establish specific conditions for legal termination. Section 3[12] of the Act acts like a saving clause and guards the medical practitioners from punishment under IPC. Furthermore, Section 4[13] talks about places where the abortion can take place.

2021 Amendments in the MTP Act –

Plethora of conflicting opinions and verdicts led to chaos and confusion which ultimately pushed the legislature to enact the *Medical Termination of Pregnancy Amendment Bill, 2020"*. The Health Ministry on the 2nd of March, presented this law, which is generally regarded as a massive step forward for the women's rights. The amended MTP Act increased the time period of getting an abortion done. Earlier, getting an opinion of one doctor was necessary to get abortion done withing twelve weeks. Further opinion of two doctors were required for termination of pregnancy within twelve to twenty weeks. The Act permits abortion up to 20 weeks on the advice of one doctor and within 20 to 24 weeks in certain cases on the advice of two doctors. The cases in which termination beyond 20 weeks and up to 24 weeks is allowed are- rape survivors, differently abled women and vulnerable women. The Act creates state - level Medical Boards to evaluate the abortion after period of 24 weeks if significant foetal deformities exist. Further, the MTP Amended Act replaces "by any married women or husband" to "any women or her partner'. The amended Act constitutes a Medical Board which shall include practitioners from various medical fields like gynaecology, paediatrician etc."[14] Also as per *Section 5(A) 1[15]*, the name and personal information of women should not get revealed while termination of her pregnancy and further not following it will lead to liable under *Section 5(A) 2[16]*with imprisonment up to one year or fine or both.

This can be further explained through a case "***Mahima Yadav v. Government of NCT of Delhi and others"[17]***. The factual matrix is that Mahima Yadav filed a petition for permission to get its foetus medically terminated even though her foetus was about 25 weeks old. The petitioner here alleges that, she should be allowed to get terminated this foetus as she is suffering from some heart issues and also some severe hearing issue.

The Court held that as per *Section 3[18] of the Act,* termination of foetus can be allowed even after the permitted week i.e., 24 weeks in case of substantial abnormalities. In this case the High Court ordered to appoint a Board of Directors so that the petitioner i.e., Mahima Yadav could be examined. After medical examination it was held that the women is a chronic heart sufferer and is facing issue in her foetus. On this she was allowed for abortion. The court also looked over various earlier judgements like *Shaikh Ayesha Khatoon's case[19]*, *Nisha Suresh Aalam's case[20]*, *Priyanka Shukla's case[21]*. In these cases, medical termination was allowed even after 20 weeks' time period which was prevailing at that particular time period.

Amendments in the Act: -

1. Increase in gestation period –

With a development in medical technologies, now women can undergo medical termination even after the first trimester i.e. , 12 weeks. Earlier, as per the Medical Termination of Pregnancy Act, 1971 (MTP Act, 1971) any women who undergoes abortion after 20 weeks, the she should file a writ petition under the High Court or Supreme Court. But now after the amendment in the MTP Act the women can undergo termination till 24 weeks of pregnancy by taking advice of two doctors.

2. Accepting pregnancy without any traditional marriage –

With the amendment in MTP Act, now the definition has changed from "Pregnant married women" to "Pregnant Women" and also from "her Husband" to "her Partner". These minor changes will bring a positive approach to the society. These changes made in definition as per the amended MTP Act states that now even the pregnancy cases without having any traditional marriage will be considered legal. It means that unlike earlier, now there is no any need to use grievous risk as a ground of abortion but even unwanted pregnancies can be a simple ground of abortion. Similarly, Explanation 2 of Section 3 (2)[22] of the Act allows rape survivors to terminate pregnancy on the ground of mental pain due to the same.

3. Setting up Medical Boards –

Another amendment that took place in the Act is that now if the termination takes place after 24 week, then there is no necessity that High Court or Supreme Court, should issue a writ but the Honourable Court sets up Board of Directors to look after several requirements or any examination. This was also followed in case of "*Mahima Yadav v. Government of NCT of Delhi and others*"[23] where the members of the Board of Director were appointed to examine Mahima Yadav and accordingly provide a report.

Advantages of the Act: -

- Increase in gestation period from 20 weeks to 24 weeks and even above in some special cases.
- With this amended act, now the rape victim or any seek women can undergo medical termination legally.
- The Act extends to unmarried women unlike the 1971 Act that precluded them. The Act not only allows them to abort but also preserves their privacy.
- Also, this act sets up Boards of Directors to look after the problems faced by women's after 24 weeks of gestation period.

Some Issues in the Act: -

- As per section 3[24] an opinion of doctor is still necessary for getting an abortion done as per the amended Medical Termination Act. The decision for getting abortion done still does not comes under the hands of women or her partner. Apex Court also in case of *Suchita Srivastava v. Chandigarh Administration*[25]highlighted that reproductive choice of a woman is a dimension of personal liberty under Article 21.
- Another issue in the amended Act is that termination could only be done if it continues to be dangerous to the mental and physical wellbeing of the women.[26]
- Abortion beyond 24 weeks period can only be allowed if the pregnancy involves *"substantial foetal abnormalities"*. And if "*foetal abnormalities*" are involved then the women still need to file writ petition before the court of law.

Analysis and Conclusion –

When it tends to come to reproductive rights, India has legislation in place. Around 40% of the pregnant women lives in a total of 125 countries, where either the abortion is prohibited or if permitted then only to the extent to save the life of women.[27] Though this amendment is a stepping stone towards regulating abortion, the authorities must ensure that all medical practise and standardised protocols for termination should be followed at every health care facility around the world and also the decision should be taken following Human Rights and Sound Scientific Principals. Now, after several amendments of the Act, the act though not fully but still is working good for the society by increasing the time of termination.

References:

[1] Indian Penal Code § 312 (1860).

[2] Bela Ganata and others, Global, Regional, and Subregional Classification of Abortions by Safety

[3]https://www.ncbi.nlm.nih.gov/pmc/ - accessed on 04th March, 2022

[4] Indian Penal Code § 312-316 (1860).

[5] Indian Medical Council Act (1956)

[6] Medical Termination of Pregnancy Act (2021).

[7] Medical Termination of Pregnancy Act (1971).

[8] Medical Termination of Pregnancy Act § 3 (2021).

[9] Indian Penal Code § 312-316 (1860).

[10] Medical Termination of Pregnancy Act (1971).
[11] Medical Termination of Pregnancy Act § 312 (IPC 1876).
[12]*Supra 8*
[13] Medical Termination of Pregnancy Act § 4 (2021).
[14] Medical Termination of Pregnancy Act § 3 (2C) (2021).
[15] Medical Termination of Pregnancy Act § 5 (A)1 (2021).
[16] Medical Termination of Pregnancy Act § 5 (A)2 (2021).
[17] Mahima Yadav v. Government of NCT of Delhi and Ors., (2021).
[18]*Supra 8*
[19] Shaikh Ayesha Khatooon v. Union of India and Ors., (2018).
[20] Nisha Suresh Aalam v. Union of India & Ors., (2018)
[21] Priyanka Shukla v. Union of India and Ors., (2019)
[22] Medical Termination of Pregnancy Act § 3(2) Explanation 2, (2021).
[23]*Supra 17*
[24]*Supra 8*
[25] Suchita Srivastava v. Chandigarh Administration, (2009)
[26] Medical Termination of Pregnancy Act § 3(2)(1), (1971).
[27]https://www.guttmacher.org/report/abortion-worldwide-2017

CHAPTER NINE

A STUDY ON THE LIABILITY OF MEDICAL PROFESSIONALS FOR NEGLIGENCE

Maitreyi Shishir*

**4th Year, BA LLB, Symbiosis Law School, Hyderabad*

Introduction and Scope

Negligence does not have a definite meaning. However, it can be considered as an act done recklessly which causes others unforeseeable damages[1]. It includes the omission of any act that a reasonable man would do or the commission of an act that a reasonable man would not do.[2] Whether an act was done in a negligent manner or not can be understood by the circumstances and the knowledge of the involved parties. Negligence has been considered as an offense under various Indian laws including the Penal laws, Contract Laws and many more.

Medical Negligence is said to be an act that is done without proper care which causes a breach in their duty leading to harm to the patient. This concept is based on the idea that any medical professional can be deemed to be an expert in the task they have taken up. When a patient takes their services, they are certain that the medical professional shall act in accordance to certain standards of care. However, when the medical professional, due to his recklessness, harms the patient, he should face certain legal consequences for the same.

When a medical professional causes a mishap due to his negligence, the consequences could be a minor hurt to a fatal risk, even causing death. A medical professional is a human, and therefore making any mistake is only humane. However, to cause such consequences, not due to a mistake but instead due to a chosen negligence is unacceptable. The very basis for considering an act as Medical Negligence is the willful neglect that any professional causes maybe during a procedure, operation, diagnosis, or even the injecting of anesthesia.

If we have to establish the essentials of Medical Negligence, it would include:

The omission of an act a reasonable ma would do OR the commission of ac act a reasonable man would not do

This act OR omission leads to an unforeseeable harm

This basically means that an omission or act would only be considered negligence if it leads to harm to the plaintiff directly.[3]

When the prestigious Harvard University did a study on medical malpractice cases in India, it was found out that almost 5 million people die in India each year due to medical negligence.[4] This shows the alarming amount of people that have suffered due to the negligence of a medical professional. This has made this a very serious issue for our country. Even though medical professionals are considered a form of God in India, they have been causing enough harm to raise an alarm. Their mistakes have been stemmed from a lack of experience and knowledge to mere negligence. Therefore, the laws and the Court have become very active in protecting the rights of its citizens.

Every medical professional has bestowed upon them a legal duty. This duty is based upon the simple fact that every patient that approaches them has come in with trusting their lives in their hands, the hands of an expert. The medical professional has specialized knowledge that no other common man has. The professional give themself an authority of expertise when they train and give medical treatment and advice to others. Therefore, it becomes their duty to carry on all acts and no omissions that any other person from his field would do.

This research shall look into the concept of Medical Negligence in India. It shall look into the various duties that have been bestowed upon the medical professionals including the duty to keep standard of care, duty to care and duty to attend their patients etc. It will then look into the liability that arises through medical negligence under various laws including Criminal law, Civil law, Consumer law etc. It shall move on then understanding all the major landmark decisions taken by the Indian Courts. Finally, an assessment shall be made on the defenses that are available to the Medical Professionals.

Research Methodology and Sources

This research shall be based on Doctrinal Legal Research Methodology. The research shall focus on studying the "Indian Penal Code"[5] and "Consumer Protection Act"[6] and their various sections to understand the liability of medical negligence on medical professionals. The nature of the study would be both descriptive and analytical in nature. Case laws shall be used to understand the practical aspects of Medical Negligence and how the courts deal with it.

This research will primarily refer to two types of sources i.e., Primary and Secondary. The primary sources that will be referred to shall be SCCOnline and Manupatra for an in-depth understanding of the landmark case laws. Secondary sources shall also be used such as various national and international journal articles, books, and various other material available on the internet.

Components of Medical Negligence

Every medical negligence case has to it some specific components. Only when such components take place, the incident is considered as one.

Duty

Doctors have been placed on a high pedestal. They are deemed as gods on earth. They have certain skills and knowledge that deal with the lives of people. They, therefore, have a huge obligation on them which puts on them a one-sided liability. They have to always make sure that they are taking care of a person in the most reasonable and prudent manner. However, every doctor has a duty to act in accordance with that of any other doctor of his field would have. For instance, a family doctor shall not have the same duty to look after a patient as a cardiologist.

The duty of a doctor has been highlighted under various case laws as well. The judiciary has stated that "every doctor, at the governmental hospital or elsewhere, has a professional obligation to extend his services with due expertise for protecting life"[7].

Dereliction in the Duty

The next component of the negligence that has to be proved is that the duty that the medical professional had was mismanaged or misused. In other words, the duty should be breached. The doctor should have performed such an act that anyone else in his capacity in a similar position would have not done. A common principle that is applied at this stage to understand whether the act was right or wrong is to follow the principle of *res ipso loquitur.* This term comes from evidentiary law and means that "the thing speaks for itself". This means that the breach of duty that shall take place by the medical professional shall speak for itself and make it evident whether he has committed the crime or not. It shall also display very clearly that the breach was not a result from the patient in any form.

The doctor cannot give an assurance that he shall be able to cure the patient. However, he does give the assurance that he shall do everything that any other doctor of his expertise would do to cure the patient. If he fails in doing so, he is made liable. The courts have also reiterated that a doctor shall "bring to his task a reasonable degree of skill and knowledge and shall exercise a reasonable degree of care"[8].

This reasonable degree of care includes every small detail that the doctor is expected to take care of. For instance, in a certain case, it was recognized that whenever a surgery has to take place, it is the duty of the doctor to make sure that a chart is put up which explains exactly all the things the patient is allergic to and the quantity of anesthesia feasible to the patient. In this particular case, when the doctor breached his duty in doing so. The court held the doctor liable.[9]

Damage faced

This essential states that the breach that the doctor commits while exercising his duty should cause some amount of damage to the patient. This means that medical negligence can only be claimed against the doctor if the breach caused some issue to the patient. If no such damage took place, then the doctor cannot be sued even if he was incompetent in his acts. However, he can be made liable under the criminal law as per the provisions of "section 336 of the penal code"*[10]*.

The damage that the patient faces can be of any type. This includes both monetary and physiological damage:

- For aggravating a previous medical condition of the patient
- For decreasing the chances for the recovery of the patient
- For monetary expenses that the patient may face
- For causing or aggravating the pain and misery of the patient both physically and mentally
- For causing difficulties such as increasing recovery time that makes him lose his job etc. On purpose
- For making a loss of vigor
- For making the patient lose on basic life requirements such as losing his limbs
- For causing his expectations with life to reduce
- For causing his death etc.

Direct Result

The fourth essential requirement for a person to claim for medical negligence is that the damage that was caused to the patient was a direct result of the negligent manner in which the medical professional acted. It believes that to claim damage, the patient has to establish that the damages that they are facing are a proximate result of the negligent acts of the medical professional. Proximate cause refers to "a cause, which in a natural and continuous sequence, unbroken by any efficient intervening cause, produces the injury, and without which the injury would not have occurred"*[11]*.

Duties on a Medical Professional

As discussed earlier, medical professionals have entrusted on them some duties. They are supposed to make sure that these duties are followed.

Duty to constantly attend

It is an essential duty of the medical professional to constantly attend and keep a check on the patient. If any patient has been admitted to the hospital, especially in the emergency ward, and if the medical professional does not attend to the patient in a timely manner, and if through the consequences of his failure in doing so, the patient dies, he shall be held liable for being ignorant.

In a particular case, a patient had met with a road accident and was admitted to the hospital. When the senior doctor was called to look into the matter, he did not show up, even after repeated calls. The patient, later on, passed away due to a lack of medical support. The senior doctor was held liable and was made to pay damages amounting to Rs. 1, 25, 000*[12]*.

Duty to take care

Another essential duty that is bestowed upon a doctor is to give the necessary care to the patient. These duties include:

- To make a decision on whether he shall be taking his case
- To make a decision on what treatment he shall be providing him
- To make genuine and reasonable efforts towards making sure that the treatment is undergone correctly

If the doctor is incapable of following these above–mentioned duties, he shall be held liable for negligence in taking care of his patients. He shall be held liable for being incapable if he does or does not do any act that is required to be done by a medical professional in a reasonable and standard manner.

For instance, in a specific case, a child had gone through surgery and was shifted from the surgical ward to the children's ward. She had suffered through burns and was therefore not allowed to wear clothes. Therefore, to ensure her health, she was shifted to the children's ward which was the warmest area available for her. Since she had already gone through surgeries for burn wounds, she was not supposed to be exposed to the harsh realities of the weather. The doctor of the children's ward did not like her being admitted to his ward without his permission and therefore removed her from his ward. He was unable to provide any reasonable explanation as to why he acted in that manner. The doctor's negligent and heartless behavior led to the death of the child. Here, the doctor was held liable for the death of the child[13].

Duty to maintain patient confidentiality

It is a duty of a doctor to make sure that he does not discuss the patient and his health records with anyone, including the family and friends of the patient without the permission of the patient. He is supposed to maintain the confidentiality of their interaction.

However, the court has held that in certain circumstances, the doctor can break his doctor-patient confidentiality. For instance, in this case, the patient was HIV positive and was marrying someone without telling them about his disease. The doctor broke his confidentiality with the patient and let the patient's fiancé know that he was HIV positive. Here, the court held that the doctor was right in breaking his confidentiality as his act came into the exception of public interest. The patient's fiancé was at the risk of getting exposed to HIV without having the knowledge[14].

Liability

The medical negligence that is committed by a medical professional has liabilities that lie under various laws.

Criminal Liability

When we look into the penal code of India, the position of a doctor has been put on a higher pedestal. The court states that when a person commits such a negligent or rash act, that causes the death of the person, without the intention of killing him, or with the knowledge that his actions may lead to the death of the person, he shall be liable for the punishments that are given for involuntary culpable homicide[15]. Sections of the penal code also state that when a death of a person takes place due to the negligent or careless behavior of another person, he shall be imprisoned and punished with a period of 2 years in prison or with a fine or with both[16].

Criminal liability arises through even acts like the wrong amount of anesthesia administered to the patient which leads to his death. Criminal liability however requires for the patient to show that the doctor committed the negligence with malicious intent or through gross negligence[17]. In many cases, vicarious liability in criminal cases also takes place. The doctor in the case will have to be vicariously liable for any negligent mistake that may lead to death made by the staff appointed by him. The vicarious liability put on the doctor and his staff would be the same liability that is imposed under Tort Law.

Liability under Consumer Protection

For many years, there seemed to be a debate on whether the services provided by a medical professional can be brought under the defined term 'services' in the laws with relation to the protection of consumers[18]. "Deficiency in services"[19] is an act that can be provided with a remedy under COPRA. The Supreme Court however gave its take on the matter. In a landmark judgment, the court brought in medical services under the definition of services in the Act. This was brought in with the concept that patients and medical professionals had a contractual relationship, with the money being the consideration. If the medical professional failed in providing adequate services through its negligent acts that caused the injury, the patient could always sue it for the same[20].

Civil Liability

Civil Liability is the most diverse and important form of liability for medical negligence. Civil law allows for liability for medical negligence even for medical services provided free of cost. It encompasses within it, the liability that crosses the liability arising from consumer law. Whenever a patient is unable to file for a remedy against negligence under the Consumer Law due to lack of payment, they can change their course of remedy to civil law. They can claim for negligence and file for damages. However, here the burden of proof for the negligence is on the patient. He has to prove to the court that it was the direct negligence of the medical professional that led to his damages.

This liability arises over the sole fact that medical professionals have a certain set of skills and knowledge that differentiates them from the average person. When such a person decides to take in any case, with or without the acceptance of money, he provides his "implied undertaking" that he shall look into while deciding on the treatment he shall be providing and the manner in which he shall provide it.

The courts have time and again reiterated that every medical professional has to make sure that he provides his services in the most righteous amount of care and the highest degree of skills[21]. This liability however is not set to a level of impossibility. It is a well-known fact that humans cannot be perfect. Even the most educated and practiced doctor can make mistakes. A medical professional shall only be held liable for negligence if the patient can prove that the mistake made by the professional is negligence on his part as no other medical professional with the same amount of expertise and practice can make such a mistake if they also acted in a careful manner[22]. The mistake should be sourced out of negligence that no one else in his field would have made[23].

The patient has to fulfill certain necessities before filing for civil liability of medical negligence. The patient has to prove that the medical professional has done or failed to do such an act that has caused direct damages to the patient while breaching his duty. The patient is expected to prove that the medical professional is liable with the help of experts and their articles[24].

Compensatory Liability

An important factor when it comes to civil liability is the manner in which people are punished. The punishment essential looks into the compensation of the victim. If any negligent act takes place while under the supervision of a doctor or a hospital, the concept of vicarious liability steps in. They are supposed to provide the victim with compensatory remedies. Even if the staff of a hospital, who does not deal with the technical medical science, acts in a negligent manner, it is the hospital that is made liable. An example of the same would be the death of an individual due to improper cleaning of the hospital washroom. The hospital was made vicariously liable and had to make the payment of a sum of Rs. 1 lakh[25].

The courts have also shed light on the difference of liability when it comes to civil and criminal law. The courts have stated that "to impose criminal liability under Section 304-A, it is necessary that the death should have been the direct result of rash and negligent act of the accused, without other person's intervention"[26].

Disciplinary Liability

Another manner through which the courts can make sure that negligent behavior by the doctor does not take place is through taking disciplinary action against the wrongdoer. There are several laws[27] under various acts[28] that allow for the Medical Council in India to suspend the license or remove the names of any medical professional who causes misconduct.

Defense or Exceptions to Medical Negligence

Every liability that arises has its exception, there needs to remain a balance. The same goes for medical negligence. There are certain defenses that a medical professional can take for his defense.

The first defense that a medical professional has is that if anything occurs due to a natural circumstance, such as accident or misfortune, where no knowledge or malified intention was noted, while doing an act that is lawful in nature in a manner that is lawful, while making sure that all necessary precautions have been taken care off, then the medical professional is not liable[29].

The second defense is in relation to acts done in good faith. It states that when an act is being committed, without having any preconceived notion of causing any sort of injury to the patient, but with the sole intention of protecting the patient from any damages to himself, then that shall not amount to medical negligence[30].

The third defense available to a medical professional is that when an act is being committed, without having any preconceived notion of causing any sort of injury to the patient even though there exists a chance of harm, but with the sole intention of protecting the patient from any harm to himself, and that the patient himself has given him the allowance of committing such an act, in an implicit or explicit manner, then that shall not amount as medical negligence[31].

There have also been many landmark judgments for the same. The courts have held that for treating a patient for a particular illness, there are many acceptable forms of treatment. Every doctor may follow his preferred manner of treatment for the same illness. He cannot be said to be negligent just because he chose one manner of treatment that is different from others. He just needs to make sure that whatever manner of treatment he chose, he followed it and delivered the procedure with utmost care and skills. He cannot be made liable for choosing a manner of treatment*[32]*.

The Consumer Redressal Commission also stated in a judgment that every doctor is expected to perform his duties in the most careful and skillful manner. Every case differs and if his procedure fails in resolving the patient, even after putting in a reasonable amount of skill and care, he cannot be made liable for it.*[33]*

Conclusion

Every law has been made to make sure that the rights of the people remain protected. The interests and betterment of society is the utmost goal. India has a rising case of medical negligence and death caused by it. The lawmakers have therefore tried their best to protect the rights of the citizens from big and rich hospitals and doctors. They are aware of how the poor and individual patients suffer through the hands of the rich. However, a lot of times medical negligence cases have been made out of non-existential facts. Therefore, there are laws that help in protecting medical professionals from any exploitation as well. However, even today, making people aware and making them realize that there are forums to help them in case of medical negligence is difficult. People still consider doctors a form of God in many areas. What the doctor tells them is the final word and therefore they are exploited by them. A lot of times they are unable to go to courts because they are suffering from the loss of their loved ones and therefore, they do not have the presence of mind or time to go to the courts for helping them out. Medical negligence, therefore, is underutilized and it will take time for people to become aware of their rights and fight for them in the court of law.

References:

1. Annu Bahal, *Critical analysis of various Indian legislations for medical negligence.*

1. Vichar Mishra, *Forensic Medicine and Medical Jurisprudence* (2021).
2. India's medical error deaths, nearly 5 mn a year, can be cut by 50%: Expert, BUSINESS STANDARD, October 28, 2018.
3. Hrinmaya Nanda & Amruta Das, *Medical Malpractice in India: A Critical Analysis of Liability and Defense Framework*, 20 INDIAN JOURNAL OF PHYSIOLOGY 188–190.
4. Krishna S Nehra, *Medical Malpractice Liability: India*, Library of Congress (2009), https://www.loc.gov/law/help/medical-malpractice-liability/india.php.
5. Saurabh S Ranchh, *Medical Negligence in India*, Manupatra.
6. S V Joga Rao, *Medical negligence liability under the consumer protection act: A review of judicial perspective*, 25 INDIAN JOURNAL OF UROLOGY 361–371 (2009).
7. Amit Agarwal, *Medical negligence: Indian legal perspective*, 1 ANNALS OF INDIAN ACADEMY OF NEUROLOGY (2016).
8. M Jagannadhan Rao, *REPORT ON MEDICAL TREATMENT TO TERMINALLY ILL PATIENTS (PROTECTION OF PATIENTS AND MEDICAL PRACTITIONERS)* (2006), https://lawcommissionofindia.nic.in/reports/rep196.pdf.

Citations:

[1] Amit Agarwal, Medical negligence: Indian legal perspective, 1 Annals of Indian Academy of Neurology (2016).

[2] Hirnmaya Nanda & Amruta Das, Medical Malpractice in India: A Critical Analysis of Liability and Defense Framework, 20 Indian Journal of Physiology 188–190.

[3] King v. Philips, (1953) 1 QB 429

[4] India's medical error deaths, nearly 5 mn a year, can be cut by 50%: Expert, Business Standard, October 28, 2018.

[5] Indian Penal Code, 1860

[6] Consumer Protection Act, 2019

[7] Parmanand Kataria vs. Union of India , AIR 1989 SC 2039.

[8] Laxman vs. Trimback, AIR 1969 SC 128

[9] Jagdish Ram v. State of H.P., AIR 2007 (NOC) 2498 (HP)

[10] The Indian Penal Code, 1860, No. 45, Acts of Parliament, 1860 (India)

[11] Vichar Mishra, Forensic Medicine and Medical Jurisprudence (2021).

[12] Shishir Rajan Saha v. The State of Tripura, AIR 2002 Gau 102

[13] Gian Kaur v. Vinod Kumar Sharma, 1985 Crl.L.J.931

[14] Dr. Tokugha v. Apollo Hospital Enterprises Ltd., Civil Appeal No. 4641 of 1998

[15] Shiva Ram v. The State, AIR 1965 ALL 196

[16] The Indian Penal Code, § 304A, 1860, No. 45, Acts of Parliament, 1860 (India)

[17] M Jagannadhan Rao, REPORT ON MEDICAL TREATMENT TO TERMINALLY ILL PATIENTS (PROTECTION OF PATIENTS AND MEDICAL PRACTITIONERS) (2006), https://lawcommissionofindia.nic.in/reports/rep196.pdf.

[18]The Consumer Protection Act, § 1 (42), 2019, No. 35, Acts of Parliament, 2019 (India)

[19] The Consumer Protection Act, § 1 (11), 2019, No. 35, Acts of Parliament, 2019 (India)

[20] Indian Medical Association v. V P Shantha, AIR 1996 SC 550

[21] State of Haryana v. Smt Santra, AIR 2000 SC 3335

[22] Hunter v. Hanley, (1955) SLT 213

[23] Whitehouse v. Jordan, (1981) 1 ALL ER 267

[24] Dr. Lakshman Balkrishna Joshi v. Dr. Trimbak Bapu Godbole, AIR 1969 (SC) 128

[25] M. Ramesh And Co. vs State Of Andhra Pradesh, 1975 36 STC 439 AP

[26] Emperor v. Omkar Rampratap, 4 BOM LR 679

[27] The Indian Medical Council (Professional Conduct, Etiquette and Ethics) Regulations, 2002, Regulations of Parliament, 2002 (India)

[28] The Indian Medical Council Act, 1956, No. 102, Acts of Parliament, 1956 (India)

[29] The Indian Penal Code, § 80, 1860, No. 45, Acts of Parliament, 1860 (India)

[30] The Indian Penal Code, § 81, 1860, No. 45, Acts of Parliament, 1860 (India)

[31] The Indian Penal Code, § 88, 1860, No. 45, Acts of Parliament, 1860 (India)

[32] Achutrao Haribhau Khodwa & Others vs. State of Maharashtra & Others, 1996 SCC (2) 634

[33] M. Kochar vs. Ispita Seal, I (2018) CPJ 41 (NC)

CHAPTER TEN

A Study of Mental Health & Criminal Justice System in India

Arryan Mohanty*
**Symbiosis Law School, Nagpur*

Abstract

The topic of mental health has become increasingly important, especially in the COVID-19 pandemic. This research work aims to link the topic of mental health with the criminal justice system. At first glance they may look like completely unrelated subjects, but the impact they have on each other is significant.

This paper first deals with the topic of Mental Health and the Indian Society's Attitude towards it, as it is imperative to know about the view of our society on mental health before delving into its link with criminal justice. Mental Health is still stigmatised in India, and anyone who is not mentally well is termed as 'crazy' or 'mad'. Because of this stigma, many do not consult psychiatrists. Added to this is the financial burden as such facilities are quite expensive for many Indians. The paper then deals with the link between the criminal justice system and mental health, which is, at the most basic level, the concept of *mens rea* or guilty mind element, that is needed to prove a criminal act, and becomes hard to prove it if the person who committed the crime was not aware of their actions in the first place. The paper also discusses the mental health issues faced by prisoners in India, along with the specific problems experienced by female prisoners. The paper also covers the sphere of attempted suicide and its legality, a topic governed by criminal law. Finally, the paper discusses cases relevant to the topic, 'Mental Health and Criminal Justice System'.

Introduction

Recent developments and new research have led us to delve deep again into the matter of mental health and the criminal justice system's attitude towards the same. It has been proven time and again that the traditional approach to the problems of mental disability that people fake most of the time to escape liability and work is no longer effective. In fact, the approach has never been effective and has caused a lot of problems.

However, the criminal justice system is evolving and is changing its approach. These changes are pretty evident when we look and try to understand the recent cases of Mahendra K.C. and Accused 'x'. All these changes provide us with a great perspective view of the future of the criminal justice system and its approach towards mental health especially within the India jurisdiction.

Considering the delicacy of the issues that involve crimes that relate to mental health issues, it is imperative for us to consider and pursue the matter with utmost seriousness. The most important thing at the moment is to change the stereotypical approach to mental health problems. Mental health issues have also increased a tendency among people to commit suicides which also needs to be dealt with seriously.

Mental Health and Indian Society's Attitude Towards It

Nearly 1 billion individuals worldwide suffer from a mental illness, with more than 75% of those in low-income nations not receiving care or medical counseling. Nearly 3 million individuals die each year as a result of substance misuse. Every 40 seconds, someone commits suicide. By the age of 14, around half of all mental health illnesses have emerged.[1]

It is claimed that without mental health, there is no health. Mental health is a state of well-being in which each individual reaches his maximum ability, is able to cope with daily hassles, works productively and efficiently, and contributes to his own society.[2] In other words, Disturbances in a person's thinking, feeling, or behavior (or a combination of both) that imply a problem with mental function are known as mental health problems. They make social life, career, and family activities difficult or impossible.[3] This means that a person with good mental health will be able to handle stress and anxiety and will be able to work productively without having mental breakdowns. Hence, our psychological, emotional, and social well-being are all part of our mental health. This implies that it has an influence on how we feel, think, and act on a daily basis. Our mental health has an effect on how we make decisions, how we deal with stress, and how we interact with people.[4]

Mental health concerns encompass a wide range of challenges. Issues like depression, anxiety, post- traumatic stress disorder, etc. are all a part of mental health. With the world becoming virtual, and everyone striving to become the best version of themselves, mental health issues have risen a lot. Let's understand this through an example. Let's assume that a person is constantly comparing himself to others. This will reduce his confidence and self-esteem. This can even have an adverse effect on his mental health. He'll be stressed and may develop anxiety. Anxiety, if not treated at the right time will induce other serious mental disorders thereby ruining his overall health. This also explains why therapy for mental health concerns is so important. In addition to this, mental health issues occur in all age groups and across all genders.

A lot of times, people take mental health for granted and therefore do not care about it. With a lot of people raising awareness about mental health and its importance, the government has also tried its best. To enhance this awareness, the Indian government has established new platforms such as the MANAS app. In addition, the Mental Health Care Act was also amended in 2017. This amendment decriminalized the attempt to suicide in India. Changes in societal views have always influenced the law of our land. The fundamental reason for decriminalizing suicide was the realisation that an individual who attempts suicide is already in deep sorrow, despair due to mental health problems, and penalizing that person will only add to the anguish and mental torture that they are already experiencing.[5]

For a long time, psychologists and social scientists have been concerned about the decline in mental health among the typical Indian. However, in an era of rapid technological innovation and fierce employment competition, it has been one of the least discussed topics. Psychiatrists, on the other hand, are still in short supply, making it difficult to adequately treat the problem.[6]

Mental health is considered taboo in India, and it receives little attention and importance. A lot of people don't pay much attention to the mental health of the people in their friends or even their family members. They think that with time, everything would get better without any assistance. So, people don't want to discuss their issues because they have the fear of being looked down on or being judged by the society. According to research published in the Indian Journal of Psychiatry on the rate of psychological morbidities among the general public, healthcare staff, and COVID-19 patients, around half of the population was affected by the pandemic's psychological effects. The most often reported issues across studies were poor sleep quality (40%), stress (34%), and psychological discomfort (34%)[7]. However, even during this period of isolation, when the mental health issues increased, not much attention was given to it.

People dealing with mental illness are regarded as "crazy" or "mad." This is the prominent reason because of which people are reluctant to go for psychiatrists. Also, because of the stigma, people are not comfortable talking about mental health in public thereby making it difficult to seek help or treatment for it. Mental problems are also seen to be the result of inadequate self-discipline and determination. Mental health stigma, as well as a lack of accessibility, affordability, and awareness, lead to severe treatment disparities.[8] This gap is approximately 50%–60% for schizophrenia, 88 percent for depression, 97.2 percent for substance misuse, and 22 percent–95 percent for seizure disorders. The treatment gap for common mental diseases is 95%, which is greater than the 76 percent gap for severe disorders. Furthermore, special populations like orphans, homeless youth, juvenile institutions, old age homes, and many other places are at a higher risk of mental illness have received less attention.[9]

One another reason is economic burden. A lot of people who face mental illness come from lower class or middle-class families. Therapy for these issues costs a fortune. A research study revealed that the costs of treating mental illnesses sometimes put families in a financial bind. This burden was accentuated in the case of middle-aged people – who were also the most afflicted by mental diseases – because it impacts their productivity, increasing the weight not just on the person but also on the economy.[10] Mental health awareness is the need of the hour. With COVID-19 lockdown coming into view, this situation has not reduced. Now, more than before, it is important for the government and individuals to step up the game and talk openly about mental health. The stigma should be removed gradually and treatment for such problems should be encouraged as well.

Mental Health and Criminal Justice

When it comes to criminal law, one must understand the concepts of *actus reus* and *mens rea*. *Actus reus* refers to the act element of the crime; that is, a wrongful act has been committed. It is thus a bodily movement that is voluntary.[11] It needs to be supplemented by another element, that of a guilty mind or mens rea. Both *mens rea* and *actus reus* are needed to define a crime.[12] Thus, according to Lord Diplock, if *mens rea* cannot be proved, no crime has been committed.[13] This process for defining a criminal act seems quite logical and straightforward, but becomes quite complicated and even quite controversial when the actions of a mentally disabled person are considered. Proving their *mens rea* may be difficult, as it is possible that the person was not even aware of their actions, and thus their act may not be defined as a crime. The Indian Penal Code states that if an unlawful act is done by a person who could not know the nature of their act because of unsoundness of mind, cannot be termed as an offence.[14] Moreover, death penalty for crimes committed by mentally unsound people had been disallowed by a bench led by Justice NV Ramana in 2019, although he stressed the importance of this rule being used only in cases of mental illness that are extreme.[15]

But this is only the surface of the relationship between mental health and the criminal justice system. People who are mentally disabled have to struggle more in the process despite the Penal Code's provision. Due to their mental condition, they are more likely to commit crime, and thus get arrested and imprisoned. This is despite the National Human Rights Commission's Chairman's directive that the mentally disabled are not to be lodged in prisons,[16] and called for the state governments to provide them with proper care. Prisons are the worst place for a person without soundness of mind. Unhealthy and overcrowded living conditions, paired with an already placed class system in Indian prisons, where the prisoners from higher social classes tend to be treated better,[17] make for a disastrous place for many prisoners, and are amplified for the mentally disabled who need more care. According to the India Justice Report 2020,[18] roughly 25% of the Medical Staff positions in prisons are vacant in nearly half of the states and union territories. Some states like Nagaland and Uttarakhand did not have any medical officers. Given these conditions, along with isolation for most of the day, the state of mentally disabled people is bound to worsen as these are not inducive to good mental health. A study of prisoners in a Rajasthan jail by Vinod Kumar and Usha Daria[19] found that 16.1% of the prisoners experienced depressive disorder, along with 8.5% of the prisoners experiencing anxiety, and 26.3% of them experienced neurotic disorders. Overall, one in three prisoners had psychiatric disorders. Added to this is the lack of rehabilitation facilities; prisons do not tend to provide post-release support and causes problems with re-integration of society,[20] which would prove to be even harder for the mentally disabled, and can lead to higher rates of recidivism, or re-commission of crime. This further reiterates the importance of trained staff in jails, as they can help identify and remedy such disorders in a timely manner. Due to COVID-19, psychological distress has also risen amongst prisoners, largely due to worries about the safety of their family members or fellow inmates.[21]

Women prisoners have a double disadvantage when it comes to mental health in prisons; not only are the living conditions unhealthy, but they also have to face gender discrimination. A study of women prisoners revealed that most women prisoners had committed offences that were related to their in-law's cruelty, humiliation and domestic abuse by husbands.[22] The study also found that a fourth of the respondents had had a depressive episode, and 1.5% of them had inflicted self-harm. Moreover, 30% of the female prisoners had tested positive for one or more drugs. HIV and Hepatitis C is also very prevalent, due to either unprotected sex or drug abuse.[23] The study also noted that most women were not aware of their legal aid rights. It is imperative that reforms are taken place for female prisoners because of their double disadvantage, such as mental health counselling, formation of peer-support groups for prisoners, facilities to de-addict prisoners from drugs and an all-female staff cadre.

A major problem with regards to mental health in our criminal justice system is of suicide. The Prison Statistics India 2019 showed that the suicide rate amongst prisoners is twice than that of the rest of the country, with 116 prisoners committing suicide.[24] In 2020, that number jumped to 189.[25] Suicide has been a criminal offence as per Section 309 of the Indian Penal Code 1860, stating that an attempt to commit suicide is punishable by a maximum of 1 year of imprisonment.[26] However, with the Mental Healthcare Act 2017, attempt to suicide has been decriminalized as per Section 115, by assuming that a person who tries to commit suicide is under severe stress, and thus would not be tried under the Penal Code, and will receive proper care from the concerned Government.[27] Thus, it does away with the injustices of Section 309 of the Penal Code, as the Code prescribed punishment to a person who already found life to be unsatisfactory and unbearable, thus magnifying their suffering. However, it must be noted that Section 115 of the MHA 2017 does not overrule Section 306 dealing with abetment to suicide, which stays punishable.[28]

The COVID-19 pandemic has worsened the deterioration of mental health faced by prisoners, given the need to isolate, and the fear and anxiety it brings with regards to contracting it. Moreover, it prevents inmates from consulting the medical staff safely. The Government thus came up with guidelines related to the use of telepsychiatry, to be followed when an inmate needs to consult a specialist. This includes a direct to patient video conferencing strategy, and collaborative video consultations which would have some medical staff on the patient's end as an intermediary.[29]

Relevant Cases

When we talk about the mental health scenario in India and the Criminal Justice System's approach towards it, it becomes imperative for us to consider many relevant cases that have been heard and diligently disposed of by the hon' Supreme Court and other hon' High Courts. These cases provide us with the gist of the idea behind the relationship between criminal activities and mental health disabilities. Mental health disorders have become a major and perhaps the most important reason behind suicides not just in India but all over the world. A person suffering from mental disability must be taken care of and treated with love regardless of the fact whether he/she committed a crime or not. In this section we will be discussing about a few significant cases which act as guiding authorities when it comes to the interpretation of mental health disorders and disabilities in the light of Criminal Justice System in India.

MAHENDRA K.C. v. THE STATE OF KARNATAKA AND ORS.[30]

In this case, the appellant's brother worked as driver for the accused who happened to be an officer for the State of Karnataka. The deceased had committed suicide and had left a note stating the reason for the same. The note was also posted on his social media account by the deceased himself. He posted it on Facebook and committed suicide thereafter. The note read that the accused employed various illegal means to earn wealth. He was engaged in many illegal ways of earning money and accumulate wealth. Then the accused used to transfer all of his black money to the deceased bank account to turn them white money. Thereafter, he used to transfer all the money that he transferred to the deceased bank account to his relatives' accounts. It has been alleged by the appellant that the accused threatened the deceased to kill him and caused a great deal of trauma and stress to him. This made the driver take his own life by consuming poison.

When the matter reached the Karnataka High Court, it was quashed by the single judge bench on the ground that it was a clear wastage of time and if heard, would amount to great travesty of justice. The Hon' Apex Court held that the High Court's decision to halt the investigation was unreasonable and should not have been made for the same reason. It was not the job of High Court at this stage to act like a Trial Court and test the accuracy of facts. The High Court had also crossed the limits that come with section 482 of the Code of Criminal Procedure. Moreover, the High Court did not examine the accuracy of facts either. It just went on to state its own perception of the case. The Supreme Court held that this cannot be looked upon with a "one size fits all" approach as the matter was very delicate. The Apex Court also reprimanded the single judge bench of the Karnataka High Court for calling the deceased a "weakling".

Finally, the division bench of Hon' Justice Dr. D. Y. Chandrachud and Hon' Justice B.V. Nagarathna set aside the High Court's Judgment and allowed the appeal of the appellant.

ACCUSED 'x' v. STATE OF MAHARASTRA[31]

In this case, the petitioner had been convicted of death penalty on the account of him raping two minor girls brutally and murdering them after the commission of the rape and also having a long history of raping other minor girls. The accused had been previously convicted for raping a nine-year-old girl and another seven-year-old girl. The mitigating circumstance presented were that the petitioner had an old mother who was dependent on him and also his age which happened to be considerably young but not as young as to absolve him from the death penalty.

The Trial, High and the Supreme Courts held him guilty and had upheld the death penalty awarded to him. Then the review petition was reopened again, this time to plead that the petitioner had become mentally unstable on the account of him being incarcerated for a plenty of years. The mental health condition of the petitioner had deteriorated considerably in the prison. The petitioner was a death row convict and this was his final chance to get his death penalty commuted. The Apex Court laid some guidelines that must be followed to determine the severity of the mental disorder with the help of a group of experts in this case. A 'Test of severity" must be taken to determine the severity of the mental illness suffered by the convict. In this case, the Court did not deem it necessary to set up a panel to determine the severity in this case as the facts and the other issues pertaining to the case had already been discussed. The Court held that the petitioner was so disturbed mentally that he won't be able to decipher the reason for which he was being hanged and it would render the whale punishment redundant as the whole purpose of the punishment will be defeated.

For this very reason, the death sentence of the accused was commuted to life imprisonment. Moreover, he was not to be allowed to live with common people in a society ever again. This judgment made India a new member of the league of nations who have recognized the right of mentally unstable people to be saved from death penalty.

Conclusion

Despite the fact that mental health and the criminal justice system are two quite different concepts, they are related in some ways. The research paper focuses on this similarity or inter-relation between mental health and criminal justice system, particularly in India. A legal perspective is included along with some relevant judgements.

The first topic covered in the research paper is related to mental health. This part focuses on numerous definitions and meanings of mental health. Since the topic is limited to Indian Jurisdiction, the perspective of Indian society and its outlook towards the notion of mental health has been dealt with. It is very clear that the prime reason for rise in mental health problems is stigma or taboo around this concept of mental health. Plus, there is a treatment gap because of stigma, economic and financial challenges, lack of awareness, lack of availability of treatment, etc. There is a need for removal of this stigma for the betterment of the society. Some findings include:

There is a high level of stigma associated with mental health topics in India.

Prisons in India are deteriorative for prisoners' mental health, and they tend to be highly understaffed in the medical officer post.

Female prisoners have to deal with the mental health issue along with gender discrimination, and the latter tends to be the reason for causing the former.

Indian prisoners have a suicide rate double that of the rest of the population.

COVID-19 has further increased the anxiety and fear prisoners experience due to the need for isolation and worry of catching the virus.

Then the link between mental health and criminal justice has been explained. The concepts of *actus reus* and *mens rea* are expounded in order to make understanding better and comprehensible. Even though lodging people with mental disorders is against the law, one out of three prisoners has psychiatric disorders. This part of research also highlights how there is a lack of rehabilitation facilities and post- release support for prisoners. The condition of women prisoners is worst as along with bad conditions in jail, they even have to deal with gender discrimination. This further deteriorates their mental health.

Lastly, some pertinent judgments have been noted that serve as guiding authorities when it comes to the interpretation of mental health problems and impairments in the context of India's Criminal Justice System.

Some recommendations include:

Early exposure to mental health awareness and guidance, preferably from schools, can help in significantly reducing the stigma associated with it.

Provision of more medical staff and psychiatrists in prisons can help prisoners stabilise their mental health which only deteriorates in prison if unchecked.

Encouraging the formation of peer-support groups amongst prisoners as a form of group therapy which can aid in their mental health issues.

Advancing the facilities needed for distant meetings, such as video calling with family, friends and even consultations with psychiatrists can help prisoners' anxieties.

References:

[1] Rialda Kovacevic, *Mental health: lessons learned in 2020 for 2021 and forward,* World Bank Blogs, (Feb. 11, 2021), https://blogs.worldbank.org/health/mental-health-lessons-learned-2020-2021-and-forward.

[2] Shah A. et al., *Global Mental Health Needs, Services, Barriers, and Challenges,* 38, IJMH, 14, 14-15 (2009).

[3] Amy Morin, *Mental Illness Types, Symptoms, and Diagnosis,* Very Well Mind (Feb. 17, 2021), https://www.verywellmind.com/definition-of-mental-illness-4587855.

[4] Glen Xiong, *Why It's Important to Care for Your Mental Health,* Medium (Oct. 06, 2018), https://blog.doctorondemand.com/why-its-important-to-care-for-your-mental-health-834c8670b889.

[5] Jasmine Madaan, *Decriminalization of Attempt to Commit Suicide: A Guide of 15 Decades,* IPleaders (May 07, 2020), https://blog.ipleaders.in/decriminalization-attempt-commit-suicide-guide-15-decades/.

[6]Samrat Sharma, *Depression in times of Covid: One in 10 adults suffer from mental health issues in India,* India Today (Dec. 09, 2021, 05:33 p.m.), https://www.indiatoday.in/diu/story/depression-in-times-of-covid-one-in-10-adults-suffer-from-mental-health-issues-in-india-1886014-2021-12-09.

[7] Hemant Sethi, *Overcoming the taboo of mental health in India amidst the pandemic,* Financial Express (Jul. 20, 2021, 04:49 p.m.), https://www.financialexpress.com/lifestyle/health/overcoming-the-taboo-of-mental-health-in-india-amidst-the-pandemic/2294235/.

[8]Michele Mary Bernadine, *Understanding India's mental health crisis,* Ideas for India (Apr. 06, 2021), https://www.ideasforindia.in/topics/human-development/understanding-india-s-mental-health-crisis.html.

[9] Hossain M. et at., *Improving child and adolescent mental health in India: Status, services, policies, and way forward,* 61, Indian Journal of Psychiatry, 415, 415-416 (2019).

[10] *Supra* note 8.

[11] Legal Information Institute, https://www.law.cornell.edu/wex/actus_reus (last visited Jan. 19, 2022).

[12] Britannica, https://www.britannica.com/topic/mens-rea (last visited Jan. 19, 2022).

[13] R. v. Tolson, (1889) 23 QBD 168, 187.

[14] Indian Penal Code, 1860, § 84.

[15] Dhananjay Mahapatra, *India joins nations which don't execute mentally ill convicts*, Times of India (Jun. 2, 2019, 06:40 a.m.), https://timesofindia.indiatimes.com/india/india-joins-nations-which-dont-execute-mentally-ill-convicts/articleshow/69615922.cms.

[16] National Human Rights Commission, India, https://nhrc.nic.in/press-release/nhrc-directs-states-ensure-mentally-ill-persons-are-not-jailed-under-any-circumstances (last visited Jan. 19, 2022).

[17] Shubham Kashyap, *Major problems of prison system in India*, Times of India (Jan. 01, 2022, 11:45 a.m.), https://timesofindia.indiatimes.com/readersblog/shubham-kashyap/major-problems-of-prison-system-in-india-40079/.

[18] Tata Trusts, India Justice Report: Ranking States on Police, Judiciary, Prisons and Legal Aid, (2nd ed. 2021).

[19] Vinod Kumar & Usha Daria, *Psychiatric morbidity in prisoners*, 55(4) Indian J Psychiatry 366, 368 (2013).

[20] S. Manikandan & K. Jaishankar, *Recidivism among Prisoners in Tihar Jail and Contributing Factors:*

A Qualitative Study, 46 & 47 Indian J. Criminology 46, 54 (2018).

[21] Husain Himani & Apurva Kumar Pandya, *COVID-19 and prisoners in India: Most neglected population and their mental health needs*, 7 Indian J. Health Sexuality Culture 40, 44 (2021).

[22] Muktikanta Mohanty, *BEHAVIOURAL SYNDROME OF WOMEN PRISONERS IN INDIA*, 74(4) Indian Journal Political Science 639, 643 (2013).

[23]*Ibid.*

[24] Prison Statistics India 2019, National Crime Records Bureau, https://ncrb.gov.in/en/prison-statistics-india-2019 (last visited Jan. 20, 2022).

[25] Prison Statistics India 2020, National Crime Records Bureau, https://ncrb.gov.in/en/prison-statistics-india-2020 (last visited Jan. 20, 2022).

[26] Indian Penal Code, 1860, § 309.

[27] Mental Healthcare Act, 2017, § 115.

[28] L.N. Vadlamani & M. Gowda, *Practical implications of Mental Healthcare Act, 2017: Suicide and suicide attempt*, 61(4) Indian J. Psychiatry 116, 117 (2019).

[29] P.R. Hegde et al., Dealing with Mental Health Issues in Prisoners during COVID-19: A Handbook 14 (NIMHANS 2021).

[30] *Mahendra K.C. v. The State of Karnataka and Ors.*, AIR 2021 SC 5711.

[31]*Accused 'x' v. State of Maharashtra*, AIR 2019 SC 3031.

CHAPTER ELEVEN

PROSTITUTION AND SLAVERY: CAUSES AND PRACTICES OF ERADICATING IT

Muskan Singh*
*LL.M Student, Manipal University Jaipur

Introduction

In India, women are recognized as a form of goddess. Durga, Laxmi, Saraswati are the names of Indian goddess that are being worshiped by the whole society for the growth in terms of power, finance and intelligence.[1] In a country where women are worshipped and given utmost respect, there are also some ill practices that have been taken places. Prostitution is one of the taboo which still prevails in India. There are related crimes that occur due to the occupation of prostitution. Human trafficking, slavery are some other illegal practices that women have to face not only in India but all over the world. The exercising of prostitution prevails in the country from so many years. In many of the countries there are laws governing to the prostitution and slavery yet there are countries where the issue is not recognized by the government and treated women so bad. In the following assessment there will be a discussion over the problem of prostitution in India and at worldwide level. This paper will also discuss the role of laws and administration for eliminating such problem. Another problem which is similar to the prostitution is "slavery". A slave is a person who have deprived all his rights and the life of such person is controlled by anyone else. There are different forms of slavery in India which is followed by the people that are also mentioned in the paper. The author have attempted to discussed forced labour and Forced Marriages and Sex as different type of slavery. The author have mentioned the laws by which Indian government have attempted to stop slavery from Indian. The role of Children in the cycle of slavery is also given emphasis in the paper. After the analysis of the paper there will be a brief conclusion of the findings of the research.

Prostitution

Prostitution is a profession where a person indulged in sexual intercourse with the intention of getting money in the sense of consideration. Both male and females are indulge in the profession, it is generally a not a gender specific profession. Those people who are carrying this occupation for earning their living is known as prostitutes. In India there is a general practices of calling prostitutes as "roadside brothels". in foreign countries prostitutes are known as sex workers, many of the individuals are indulged in the profession for full time and earning their livelihood respectfully. In many countries brothels are run openly in the society, which is also registered in the governmental website and paying taxes as well.[2] Many of the foreign countries accepts prostitutions as a full time business yet this practice is not accepted in India so easily. On the other hand there are some countries where prostitution is regarded as a sinful activity and considered totally unethical and illegal. Human trafficking is caused by prostitution, and most women are victims of such illegal trafficking activities. India's central government has enacted and attempted to enact and enforce legislation to prevent illegal trade and prostitution, but it is difficult to implement because many of our countries suffer from poverty, illiteracy and hunger. Problems like this have been especially common in the past.[3]

There are many factors which traps an individual into the profession of prostitution, including: Bad company, lack of education and childhood, and even lack of sex education. Lack of resources, sexual assault, psychological causes, perceptions, someone in the family involved in prostitution, etc. Prostitution not only contributes to the problem of trafficking, but can also cause a variety of health problems for consumers and prostitutes. It is very common the prostitutes suffers from sex diseases like HIV aids, STDs, Brain disorders, physiological injuries, brain trauma, cervical cancer and many more. Many of the prostitutes have died due to such diseases. In addition to that the children of prostitutes also suffers same health diseases. It is clear that prostitution have led to many disasters in the lives of people. Not only the concern person yet the whole family of the prostitute suffers from the ill tag and diseases as well. Hence, for solving such problem the Indian legislation have attempted to solve the problem by making various rules and regulations that are as follows.[4]

Laws Relating to Prostitution

There are many laws made after watching the problem of rising and illegal prostitution in India. It is seen that such laws are being enforced for saving women and men from the trap of prostitution. There are many of the women who are forced to indulged in the sexual relation with other men for the consideration of money. Few of the laws are mentioned below that:-

- **Immoral Traffic (Prevention) Act 1956**

The Act of 1956, made for the prevention of immoral trafficking and for stopping the problem of human trafficking in India. Talking over to the Indian scenario it is found that the Indian government have explicitly recognized prostitution illegal however, the Indian courts have state that prostitution is an unethical activity which shall not prevail in the society. There are so many laws that made prostitution illegal such as "Immoral Traffic (Prevention) Act 1956", as per the provisions of the Act, children and minors are not allowed to indulge in any kind of activities related to prostitution. Similarly, unsound mind people are also safeguard by the provisions of the Act. It is seen that any adult forcing or making minors/children/unsound mind individuals enters into any activity related to prostitution is liable for compensation as well as punishment. There are many other provision in the Act such as running or establishing any sex racquet is illegal yet activities related to prostitution done in a private area with free consent of all the parties involve might not be considered as illegal.[5]

The Act aims to brings decency in the society, as well as safeguard those people whom are trapped in the world of prostitution. The Act have criminalize various activities and given freedom to individuals for coming out of the world of forced sex. The Act has given power to the central government to establish fast track courts of the trial of such offenses. The Act has also given power to detect and eradicate sex hubs, brothels and so on. The Act also gives the power to the police authorities to arrest any individual whom are engaged in the criminal activities relating running or establishing brothels.

- **Article 21 of the Indian Constitution**

It is shall be known to every individual of India that Article 21 of the Constitution provide right to life and personal liberty to its people. Similarly, prostitute male or females are also the citizens of India, they are also protected under such powers of the Constitution. Right to life also includes right to live with dignity, that gives the power to women to fight for themselves and save themselves from forced sex. After revising the condition of such women, the government has taken the step of making educational and training institutions to save them from the line of poverty. Therein, as per Article 21 of the Constitution, all the prostitutes has the right to maintain a dignified life and it is the duty of government to ensure livelihood of such trapped people in India. Moreover, the society also plays a significant role here that they shall also respect the people and shows a humble attitude, not pulling them back from where they are trying to be free.[6]

Causes of Prostitution

There are many aspects by which women are forced to enter into the world of prostitution. Majority of the women are not willing to work as a prostitute but have no other option to fulfill their needs and wants. Unemployment and poverty are the two major factors because of which women are inkling towards the profession of prostitution. It is seen that there are so many intermediate people who tries to influence women and offers jobs related to prostitution. Poverty is the biggest reason of prostitution; a mother will go to any way for feeding her child. Many a times it is found that women indulging in sexual intercourse for money are doing it for feeding themselves as well as their family. Yet it is a one way road and there is no coming back from the profession.[7]

Another factor that leads to prostitution is unemployment. Women that are not educated and have no other skills are also influenced to pursue such profession. Increasing unemployment is giving rise to prostitution, where women think of earning more money in very short span of time. Whereas, there is a major role of kidnapping in the field of prostitution. It is found that women at very young age are being kidnapped by the gangs and forced for having illicit relation with men. In villages it is also a tradition to buy a woman in order to get married. There are many villages where there is a huge gender ratio gap. Number of women is very less compared to men. Hence, at such places women are kidnapped from different sates and sold to men for marriage or any other purposes. Moreover, kids that are kidnapped at very early ages and sent for begging till maturity age. Afterwards, girls are sent to the brothels as a sex worker. The situation gets so worst when the children of such people are also forced to enter into the same field. Those women who are forced to work as a prostitute can also file criminal complaint for rape under section 375 of the Indian Penal Code, 1860.

Slavery

In general terms a slave is considered as an individual who is owned by any other individual and waived off all his/her basic freedom and rights. Slavery can be done for many purposes, it can be done for labors, chattel slavery and so on. A slave is a person who have deprived all his rights and the life of such person is controlled by any one else.[8] The owner will decide the rights and freedom which a slave can enjoy. The system of slavery is not new but running from ancient period of time. Men and women were hired as slaves for a lifetime period. In the ancient period it was found that the king who concur any other kingdom have the right to make soldiers and their family to employed as slaves. Similarly, in India as well the term slavery is not new and running from a long period of time. The king's rule had always promoted the slavery patters after winning battles.[9]

There are different types of slavery that are running in the Indian societies and these are as follows:-

- **Forced labor**

It is a kind of slavery where the labors are forced to work under pathetic conditions. They work under stress, duress and also after various types of threats and coercion. The majority of the forced labor belongs to very young age people that are easy to brain wash and compel for doing any kind of work. Many of the children are forced to work for preying their families, they are sent to work by the parents with the view of earning basic wages so that they can at least avail day meal. Boys are often taken by their fathers in the factories and construction sites so that they can learn the work fast and easily. On the other hand girls are taught dancing and music at a young age so that they can work on the entertainment industry for the kinds and their ministers in the ancient period. Children are deprived of education hence, after becoming adults they are left with no choice other then slavery. Moreover, there was a trend that if the parents have not paid their debts on time, their children, after the expiry period, when the parents are not able to pay their debts, their kids are kept as slaves.[10]

- **Forced Marriages and Sex Slavery**

In India this kind of slavery is very common. Moreover, in some of the religious countries this practice is also very common where women and teenage girls are sold to older men or forced to marry older men whom are having good status in the society. This practice is very common in Indian villages. Such women are married to older men in order to give them a good life. However, in reality it becomes very harsh for such women to maintain the marriage and early pregnancy. The joy of life comes to an end in such marriages and they became sex slaves of their husbands. They are physically and sexually abused by the husbands and their in-laws. Afterwards, they are forced to give birth to male child, if before delivery it is found that the child will be a girl, there is a very high chance of female foeticide.[11]

Legal Provisions on Slavery in India

It is a very bright step of the Indian government to make slavery illegal in India. The bonded labour system was so common in India and there were no solution arising out of managing the situation. After some analysis the government came up with the "Bonded Labour System Abolition Act of 1976", where there are provisions added by the government that anybody found in engaging with keeping any of the men or women in bonded labour will be liable of fine as well as imprisonment upto 3 years.[12] Section 5 of the Act states that "that if there is any custom or agreement which exists for any of the bonded labour will be considered void and out of order". The very Act have helped a lot of bonded labours and made their life easy. There are similar provisions added in different Act in order to prevent bonded labour in the society such as section 3 of the "Child Labour (Prohibition and Regulation) Act, 1986 provides that no child shall be employed in forbidden from any occupations and processes".

"Section 14 of the Child Labour (Prohibition and Regulation) Act 1986, punishes any person who did not comply with the provisions of Section 3, with sentence up-to 2 years and fine up-to 20000 rupees".[13] Section 370 of the Indian Penal Code, 1860 also deals with the guidelines of bonded labors. The provision stated that any person who sells or receive any kind of money or consideration for the actoivity of bonded labour amounts to imprisonment and penalty as well. Section 358 deals with the provisions of cruelty towards slaves it states that "Assault or criminal force on grave provocation.—Whoever assaults or uses criminal force to any person on grave and sudden provocation given by that person, shall be punished with simple imprisonment for a term which may extend to one month, or with fine which may extend to two hundred rupees, or with both".[14]

Conclusion

After the deep discussion of the topic it is humbly concluded that prostitution is a profession where a person indulged in sexual intercourse with the intention of getting money in the sense of consideration. Both male and females are indulge in the profession, it is generally a not a gender specific profession. . Many of the foreign countries accepts prostitutions as a full time business yet this practice is not accepted in India so easily. It is very common the prostitutes suffers from sex diseases like HIV aids, STDs, Brain disorders, physiological injuries, brain trauma, cervical cancer and many more. Not only the concern person yet the whole family of the prostitute suffers from the ill tag and diseases as well. Hence, for solving such problem the Indian legislation have attempted to solve the problem by making various rules and regulations such as:- The Act of 1956, made for the prevention of immoral trafficking and for stopping the problem of human trafficking in India.

"Immoral Traffic (Prevention) Act 1956", as per the provisions of the Act, children and minors are not allowed to indulge in any kind of activities related to prostitution. Similarly, unsound mind people are also safeguard by the provisions of the Act. It is seen that any adult forcing or making minors/children/unsound mind individuals enters into any activity related to prostitution is liable for compensation as well as punishment. The Act aims to brings decency in the society, as well as safeguard those people whom are trapped in the world of prostitution.

Prostitute male or females are also the citizens of India, they are also protected under such powers of the Constitution. Right to life also includes right to live with dignity, that gives the power to women to fight for themselves and save themselves from forced sex. As per Article 21 of the Constitution, all the prostitutes has the right to maintain a dignified life and it is the duty of government to ensure livelihood of such trapped people in India. There are many aspects by which women are forced to enter into the world of prostitution. Majority of the women are not willing to work as a prostitute but have no other option to fulfill their needs and wants. Unemployment and poverty are the two major factors because of which women are inkling towards the profession of prostitution. Other then prostitution the other form of human trafficking is also slavery. . A slave is a person who have deprived all his rights and the life of such person is controlled by any one else. The owner will decide the rights and freedom which a slave can enjoy. There are different types of slavery that are running in the Indian societies such as forced labors and Forced Marriages and Sex Slavery. In marriage and sex slavery women and teenage girls are sold to older men or forced to marry older men whom are having good status in the society. This practice is very common in Indian villages.

References:

[1] Shingal, Ankur. "The devadasi system: Temple prostitution in India." *UCLA Women's LJ* 22 (2015): 107.

[2] Pillai, T. Vikraman. "Prostitution in India." *Indian Journal of Social Work* 43.3 (1982): 313-21.

[3] Tiwari, Reetika Raj. "Socio-Legal Analysis of Prostitution in India." *Jus Corpus LJ* 1 (2020): 155.

[4] Subramanian, Rajeshwari. "Formalisation of labour: The economics of prostitution in India." *PEOPLE: International Journal of Social Sciences* 4.2 (2018): 288-303.

[5] Bhandari, Aastha. "A Critique of the Abolitionist Approach to Regulate Prostitution in India."

[6] Sharma, Rishav, and Ujjwal Kumar Singh. "WHETHER PROSTITUTION SHALL BE LEGALISED AND REGULARISED IN FURTHERANCE OF ARTICLE 14, 19 AND 21 OF THE CONSTITUTION OF INDIA."

[7] Benoit, Cecilia, et al. "Prostitution stigma and its effect on the working conditions, personal lives, and health of sex workers." The Journal of Sex Research 55.4-5 (2018): 457-471.

[8] Manoharan, Saranya. *Awareness Intervention Against Modern Slavery in India: Influence of Caste Prejudice.* MS thesis. 2019.

[9] Oosterhoff, P., Yunus, R., Jensen, C., Somerwell, F., & Pocock, N. (2018). Modern slavery prevention and responses in South Asia: An evidence map.

[10] Srivastava, Rajendra N. "Children at work, child labor and modern slavery in India: an overview." *Indian pediatrics* 56.8 (2019): 633-638.

[11] Dickson, M. A., and Hayley Warren. "A look at labor issues in the manufacturing of fashion through the perspective of human trafficking and modern-day slavery." *The Dangers of Fashion: Towards Ethical and Sustainable Solutions* (2020): 103-124.

[12] Bonded Labour System Abolition Act of 1976

[13] Child Labour (Prohibition and Regulation) Act 1986

[14] Section 358, Indian Penal Code, 1860.

CHAPTER TWELVE

CRITICAL ANALYSIS OF MADHYA PRADESH PANCHAYAT ACT, 1993

Divyansh Bhargava* & Anshul Natani**

Symbiosis Law School, Noida

FORE School of Management, New Delhi

INTRODUCTION

The 73rd Constitution Amendment Act, 1992 has included another Part IX comprising of 16 Articles i.e. Article 243A- Article 243O and the XI Schedule to the Constitution which covered 29 subjects. The 73rd Amendment conceives the Gram Sabha as the establishment of the Panchayat Raj System to perform works and powers endowed to it by the State Legislatures. The amendment accommodates a three level Panchayat Raj System at the village, Janpad and district or Zila levels this arrangement got the consistency in the Panchayati Raj structure in India. Be that as it may, the states which were having population under 20 Lakh were given a choice to not to have the Janpad level. All the members from these three level i.e. village, Janpad, and District or Zila are chosen. Further, the chairman of Panchayats at the Janpad level and at the Zila level are chose indirectly from among the chosen members. Yet, at the village level, the appointment of chairman of Panchayat (Sarpanch) might be direct or indirect as given by the state in its own Panchayati Raj Act. Articles 243A gives that the Gram Sabha may utilize such power and perform such functions at the village level as the Legislature of a state might bė law give. The 73rd constitution amendment act, 1992 accordingly visualizes the Gram Sabha as the establishment of Panchayat Raj System. "Gram Sabha" signifies a body comprising of people enlisted in the constituent rolls included inside the territory of Panchayat at the village level. In the Panchayati Raj System Gram Sabha is the solely lasting unit. Tenure of Panchayat for example Mukhiyas and other individuals or members from Panchayat proceed for a 5 year only from the date delegated for the first sitting, however the village people don't change."

"This 73rd constitution amendment act, 1992 executes the article 40 of the DPSP which says that "State shall take steps to organize village Panchayats and endow them with such powers and authority as may be necessary to enable them to function as units of self-government" and have overhauled/upgraded them from non-legitimate to reasonable aspect of the constitution and has put constitutional devoir/obligation upon states to authorize the Panchayati Raj Acts according to provisions of the Part IX. Notwithstanding, states have been given enough opportunity to take their geographical, politico-administrative and others circumstances into account while receiving the Panchayati Raj System.[1]"

There is an arrangement of reservation of seats for SCs and STs at every level of Panchayat. The seats are to be held for SCs and STs in ratio to their populace at each level. Out of the Reserved Seats, 1/3rd must be reserved for the women's of the SC and ST. Out of the total number of seats to be filled by the direct elections, 1/3rd must be saved for women's. There has been an amendment bill in under consideration that tries to amplify for women to 50%. The reserved seats might be assigned by rotation to various constituencies in the Panchayat. The State legislature by law may likewise provide reservation for the chairperson's office."

In 2016 central government increase the reservation for women in Panchayats from 33% to 50% and in Madhya Pradesh 50% reservation for women in Panchayati Raj Institutions has already follow.[2]""

MADHYA PRADESH PANCHAYAT ACT, 1993 OVERVIEW

The 73rd Constitutional Amendment Act of 1992 gave just the fundamental structures and the rules needed for the foundation of the Panchayat Raj system, leaving the rest for the states to choose. If we talk in other words, it became obligation of the states to draft their own acts as indicated by the circumstances prevailing in the states. The legislature of Madhya Pradesh was the first to enact the Panchayat Raj Act to execute the system. Nevertheless, even after the pass of 12 years, it is as yet exploring different avenues regarding and attempting to discover with respect to what can be the ideal type of Panchayat Raj in Madhya Pradesh. In this search various amendments have occurred in the Act and the process is still on. The practical problems in executing the principally drafted provisions of the act; political aspirations of the delegates/representatives, objectives and the fallouts; political reasoning and ideology of the party in power; and the process itself are a few of the reasons liable for this long testing phase of Panchayat Raj in Madhya Pradesh."

On 1st November, 1956 new state of Madhya Pradesh was constituted, acquired a differing enactment as to constitution, functions, powers and funds of Panchayats, made in previous regions converged in the new state. The Mahakoshal region which shaped an aspect of the previous Madhya Pradesh before re-association of states, and prior to that a piece of Central Provinces furthermore, Berar Province of the British system, had well and since a long time ago settled customs in the field of city or municipal government, while improvements in former states of Bhopal, Vindhya Pradesh and Madhya Bharat, had not occurred in any effectively thought out way. The Panchayati Raj Institutions didn't follow general stance aside from toward all universal suffrage, cancelation of public electorate also, the acknowledgment of the standard of Panchayati Raj. The various constituents which constituted the new state, before re-association, had presented enactment in their concerned regions, however little advancement was recorded toward democratic based decentralization in the feudal institutional system."

The powers and functions of village or Gram Panchayats were administered by the accompanying enactments in activity in various constituent units that were converged in the new state of Madhya Pradesh

1. The Central Provinces and Berar Village Panchayats Act of 1946, as amended in 1947, 1948, 1949, 1950 and 1953.
2. The Madhya Bharat Panchayat Act 1949, as amended in 1950, 51 and 53.
3. The Vindhya Pradesh Panchayat Act, 1949
4. Bhopal State Panchayat Raj Act, 1953"

The Madhya Pradesh Panchayat Act, 1962, which was the first enactment in the re consolidated state in the field, given a 3-level arrangement of Panchayat Raj at the village level, block and district level, however the Act couldn't accomplish much without a well known base. The Act was repealed in 1981, however the new Act superseding it was viewed as a retrograde step, as it had dropped the Gram Sabha and had removed a portion of the elements of Janapad Panchayat at the Block level and Zila Panchayat at the district level. The Madhya Pradesh Panchayat Raj Act, 1990, which should be a reformed over the 1981 Act, couldn't make a lot of advance in the field of local self-government, as no elections were held at regular intervals and no authentic move of functions could occur. The experience picked up in the state, as somewhere else, during the time of 40 years, preceding the 73rd Constitutional Amendment, has exhibited that simple wanting for majority rule or democratic decentralization was insufficient. To be effective, decentralization must be upheld up by solid political will, right type of institutional system, sold practices, essential specialized and administrative endorsement and right type of attitudinal alterations in the bumbledom or bureaucracy. Every one of these essentials was missing, by and large."

Madhya Pradesh Government in the country was the 1st state who enacted the Madhya Pradesh Panchayat Raj Adhiniyam in 1993, According to the provisions of the 73rd constitutional Amendment Act, 1992. According to the 73rd constitutional Amendment Act at three level village, Janpad and district or Zila levels there is a establishment of Gram Panchayat, Janpad Panchayat and Zila Panchayat respectively.[3] The objective of the Madhya Pradesh Panchayat Raj Adhiniyam, 1993 is to merging and correcting the law identifying with the foundation of Panchayats, for guaranteeing powerful association of Panchayats in local administration and formative exercises". The Act has been changed a certain times to defeat challenges looked in its execution and furthermore for making enhancements in the light of involvement picked up."

The provisions of Madhya Pradesh Raj (sanshodhan) Adhiniynam, 2001 shall not apply to the scheduled areas so far they are inconsistent with the provisions of Chapter- XIV-A of the Act and the provisions of "The Panchayats (Extension to the Scheduled Areas) Act, 1996 (PESA)".

PANCHAYATI RAJ INSTITUTIONS IN MADHYA PRADESH

S.NO - PANCHAYATS - NO. OF PANCHAYATI RAJ INSTITUTIONS[4]

1. - Gram Panchayat - 23,922
2. - Janpad Panchayat - 313
3. - Zila Panchayat - 52

1. GRAM PANCHYAT (TV-54903)

A Gram Panchayat is established for each village. It comprises of chose Panchs and a Sarpanch, who is the chief of the Gram Panchayat. Every Gram Panchayat region is separated into at least ten and not in excess of twenty wards. Wards are regional electorates of the Gram Panchayat. A panch is chosen from each ward. The Gram Sabha is an overall body, while the Gram Panchayat is a executive, chosen body. The executive or Gram Panchayat needs to play out its obligations according to bearings given by the general body or Gram Sabha.""

2. GRAM SABHA

There is a Gram Sabha[5] for each village. The Gram Sabha comprises of the people who are enrolled in the list of electors of a village. The essential way of thinking that underlies the idea of Gram Sabha is that of democracy. Gram Sabha's give a nearby stage to individuals to meet and talk about local improvement issues and examine the growth and administrative functions of chose delegates, consequently insuring transparency or limpidity and responsibility. In particular, a Gram Sabha gives an occasion for the participation of all segments of the village such as dalits, tribals, women and other underestimated community in arranging and usage of local improvement programs.[6]"

The Panchayat Raj Act 1993 has given exclusive strengths to the Gram Sabha. The Gram Sabha can screen and question the working of the Gram Panchayat. The Panchayat Act,1993 additionally gives that Gram Sabha's can make yearly arrangements for the villages to be passed onto more higher levels of Panchayati Raj Institutions for joining. It can likewise actualize its own choices (without relying upon the Gram Panchayat) for schemes esteemed at not as much as Rs 3 lakhs."

The law requires that in any event four sessions of the Gram Sabha be held each year, in the months of January, April, July and October.[7] Extra sittings or sessions of the Gram Sabha can likewise be sorted out contingent on public needs. The Secretary[8] of the Gram Sabha assembles these sittings. The Gram Sabha session is managed by the Sarpanch[9] and in their non-appearance by the Up-Sarpanch. In the event of Gram Sabha sessions in Scheduled Areas, these are presided by a Gram Sabha member concerning to a Scheduled Tribe, who is chosen by most of the members present in that session.[10] Sittings in Scheduled Areas are held whenever requisite."

3. JANPAD PANCHYAT

Every district is splited into blocks[11]. A Janpad Panchayat is comprised for each block. Each Janpad Panchayat comprises of members or individuals chose from smaller constituencies[12]/electorates i.e. between 10-25 individuals; all individuals of the State Legislative Assembly got back from the constituencies which completely or halfway fall inside the block; and one-fifth of the Sarpanchs in the regional region of the block on a rotational basis for a time of one year. The Sarpanchs are chosen by drawing parts. Each Janpad Panchayat is chaired by a President and Vice-President who are chosen by and from among the chosen individuals."

4. ZILA PANCHYAT

A Zila Panchayat is established for a district. It includes elect individuals from the electorates i.e. between 10-35 individuals; member from Lok Sabha, Rajya Sabha and State Legislative Assembly gotten back from the district; and all chairman's of Janpad Panchayats in the district. Each Zila Panchayat is chaired by a President and Vice-President who are chosen by and from among the chosen individuals."

SOURCES OF REVENUE

The Panchayat Act, 1993 contained arrangement for a different account of Panchayat Fund. Withdrawal of cash from this account was conceivable just with the joint mark of Sarpanch and secretary of the village Panchayat. Consequently Power to pull back cash from Panchayat Fund was given to Sarpanch while in the higher echelons for example Janpad or Zila Panchayat, withdrawal powers were given to Chief Executive Official (CEO) as it were. Individuals‘ delegates were denied this power."

In Section 77(i) of Panchayat Act, 1993, Gram Panchayats are engaged to levy 6 necessary taxes, and under section 77(2) of Panchayat Act, 1993, 14 discretionary taxes, subject to the provisions of the Act and conditions and exclusions, as might be recommended by the state government. Mandatory assessments incorporate, property charge on land and structures, lavatory charge, light duty, business charge, market expenses and charges for the registration of livestock. The income of Gram Panchayats originates from three sources which are as follows:-

i. taxes and expenses imposed and gathered under the Act,
ii. Grants-in-help from the state government, both general and explicit and,
iii. Transfer of assets from the state government or from central government on the proposals of the State Finance Commission or Central Finance Commission."

There is just a single compulsory assessment that can be imposed by Janpad Panchayats, charge on theater, dramatic shows and other public amusement. The main discretionary assessment which the Janpad Panchayats can impose is a charge for any permit or consent conceded by them for the utilization and control of land and other property of the Janpad. The Act doesn't present any tax collection powers to Zila Panchayats. The only source of revenue of Zila Panchayat is that what is given to them by the state government by virtue of land income and furthermore certain grants in-help by the state government all alone or on the proposal of the State Finance Commission."

From the Gram Panchayat in Amendment of Panchayat Act, 1997 has take back nearly all powers regarding of taxation and moved such powers to Gram Sabha, exclude two mandatory assessments from Schedule I of the prior Act, 1993 which are as follows:-

i. Market charges on individuals disclosing for marketing in any market or at any place or any building or structure having a place with Gram Panchayat.
ii. A charge for the enlistment of animals sold in the market or spot having a place with or under the monitoring of the Gram Panchayat."

Essentially, except for three discretionary expenses from schedule II of the prior Act, 1993 all other discretionary charges would now be able to be imposed by the Gram Sabha. These discretionary charges which stay with the Gram Panchayat are as follows:-

i. An duty on bullock carriage, bikes and rickshaws
ii. drainage charge where arrangement of drainage has been presented by the Gram Panchayat
iii. A charge payable by proprietors of vehicles other than motor vehicles. Before the Amendment of 1997, Gram Panchayats were engaged to levy 6 necessary taxes and 14 discretionary assessments, subject to the provisions of the Act and conditions and exceptions as might be recommended by the state government. The compulsory assessments included property charge on land and structures, a lavatory charge, light expense, calling charge, market expenses and charges for the enrollment of animals."

Two new schedules I-a containing the table of mandatory duties and Schedule II-A in regard of discretionary taxes which can be levied by Gram Sabha, have been added to the current schedule I and schedule II which have gone through generous decrease in the quantity of duties, resulting upon the amendment of the Act in 2001."

Each Gram Sabha will build up a fund or reserves to be known as the Gram Kosh, comprising of the following 4 sections:-

i. Anna Kosh
ii. Shram Kosh
iii. Vastu Kosh and
iv. Nagad Kosh.

Receipts from the accompanying sources will be credited to the Gram Kosh which are as follows:-

i. Gifts,
ii. Income from different sources,
iii. Sums got from the Gram Panchayat reserves, accompanied proceed from land income, cess on land income, pasturing charges, to be apportioned to Gram Sabha's as per the standards fixed by the State Government.
iv. Taxes levied by the Gram Sabha
v. any amount got by the Gram Panchayat under different plans supported by the central government or state government, to be distributed to Gram Sabha, according to standards endorsed by the central government or state government.

The Gram Kosh will be worked by the Gram Vikas Samiti and all sums from the reserves will be pulled back under the joint mark or sign of the Treasurer and Secretary of the Gram Vikas Samiti, with the endorsement of the Gram Sabha. The treasurer of Gram Kosh is to be designated by the Gram Vikas samiti."

The ongoing advance toward Gram Swaraj in Madhya Pradesh, giving more rights to Gram Sabha's, is expected to make Gram Panchayats as units of self government. The accomplishment of this analysis would generally rely on the way in which the amended Act is executed and various bodies made play out their performance. The amicable working of the Gram Panchayats and the Gram Sabha's and their extraordinary standing panels, is extremely fundamental for the achievement of gram Swaraj."

RIGHT TO INFORMATION AND PANCHAYATI RAJ INSTITUTIONS (PRIs)

The Right to Information put a positive obligation on governments to disperse data to the public and stretches out an option to individuals to look for and get government-held data and a few data from private bodies. Commonly, information is revealed to people in two different ways:

- **Proactively**: Government bodies are needed to effectively distribute and disperse key classes of data which are of general enthusiasm of people in general, for example, their authoritative structure, the services they provide, significant structures, decision making procedures and so forth. This information can be revealed, for instance, by notifying up notification and publish information on notice boards, promulgating information in the official gazette, perusing out information in gatherings or on the other hand promulgating reports on the web.
- **Upon Requisition**: Government bodies must set up systems to facilitate approach to explicit parts of information upon demand, including straightforward or easy, timely and inexpensive application and appeals procedure. Most generally, special officer inside public bodies are given the obligation to deal demands which are asked by the people and give acquaintance."

Distinctly, it is basic that public reserve the 'right to get to information' from Panchayats since they are simply the local self governing bodies which are nearest to the individuals. So as to encourage access, in 1997 the Government of India publish a circular in which expressing that every State ought to consider passing orders executing three distinct parts of limpidity or transparency. Firstly, Panchayati Raj Institutions, particularly Gram Panchayats, should show all important information relating to advancement ventures (particularly receipt of assets and how they are being spent) in the Panchayats workplaces or on a noticeable board outside the neighborhood school. Secondly, all significant records ought to be available to inspection.

Thirdly, individuals of the general population ought to have the option to get copies of reports relating to advancement ventures (including in specific all bills, muster rolls, vouchers, estimation, and dimension books, in addition to the economic norm and process for determination of recipients and lists of recipients), just as matters of general public rights by paying an normal charge. Commonly, these parts of transparency have been mirrored in the laws and guidelines referenced underneath, particularly in the Panchayati Raj Act of Madhya Pradesh."

Madhya Pradesh has the accompanying laws or orders set up which facilitate approach to information held by Panchayat bodies which are as follows:

- Madhya Pradesh Panchayat Raj Avam Gram Swaraj Adhiniyam, 1993;
- Executive Orders, compiled by the Department of General Administration in a book title "Janane ka Haq";
- Madhya Pradesh Jankari ki Swatantrata Adhiniyam, 2002;
- Right to Information Act, 2005.

The move towards brought together enactment or law on Panchayats in Madhya Pradesh began with an examination by the Rural Local Self-Government Committee which is set up in 1957. The end purpose of this activity was the Panchayati Raj Act of 1962. Because that time the State has amended the Panchayati Raj Act a number of times.[13] After the 73rd constitutional amendment in respect of Panchayati Raj Institutions which came into force in 1993, another Panchayat Act known as the Madhya Pradesh Panchayati Raj Adhiniyam 1993 was passed by the State Legislature on 30 December 1993 and became effective on 25 January 1994, supersedes the prior Panchayat Act of 1990.[14] An amendment in 2001 altered the name of the Act to the "Madhya Pradesh Panchayati Raj avam Gram Swaraj Adhiniyam, 1993" (Panchayati Raj Act 1993)."

It is remember able that the Panchayati Raj Institutions amendment to the Indian Constitution was not automatically apply to Schedule V areas.[15] After the Central Government passed the Provisions of the Panchayats (Extension to the Scheduled Areas) Act in 1996, nonetheless, the State Government added another chapter to the Panchayati Raj Act 1993 by a amendment in December 1997 to make exclusive rules or laws for Panchayats in Scheduled Areas in Madhya Pradesh."

The Panchayati Raj Act 1993 has various rules and regulations related explicitly to reach to information by either the overall population or by chose delegates. These rules and regulations will be examined in detail in chapter III-VII of Madhya Pradesh Panchayati Raj avam Gram Swaraj Adhiniyam 1993 (Panchayati Raj Act 1993)."

In addition to the approach provisions allowed under the Panchayat Raj Act 1993, its Rules and the Panchayati Raj Department Executive Order, Madhya Pradesh additionally has a extensive law on right to information. Actually, as far back as 1997 the Madhya Pradesh Government built up a Right to Information Bill, yet, as noted prior, subsequent to being passed by the State Assembly in 1998 which is not get Presidential Consent and was removed."

In 2002 the Madhya Pradesh Government passed a Right to Information Act which is also known as the "Madhya Pradesh Jankari ki Swatantrata Adhiniyam 2002". The Act got the consent of the Governor on 24 January 2003 and was distributed in the Madhya Pradesh Gazette (Extraordinary) on 31 January 2003.Despite the sanctioning of the Act, nonetheless, comparing Rules have still not been outlined, with the end goal that the Act has not yet been adequately operationalised."

The Act gives each citizen the right to observe and acquire duplicates of any record made in the past three years in the authority of the public body. This is a generally restricted right, as all other State laws in India put no time limit and surely not such a brief time limit on records which are accessible for approach. The Act reaches out to the whole province of Madhya Pradesh, covering 'public bodies' including all state government offices. It likewise covers all local authorities comprised under an Act of the State Legislature, which would incorporate Panchayati Raj Institutions under the Panchayat Raj Act 1993.""

The Act put a few obligations on public authorities to release some information proactively, requiring the display at least of the description of facilities peoples can use to get information."

Under the Act, information can be demanded by composing an application in writing to the "designated officer", either for overview of document or to get a duplicate of a record. In the wake of getting the application, the official should determine the application within 30 days from date of receiving an application."

After the enactment of State Information Act, 2002 by Madhya Pradesh in May 2005 central government pass the Right to Information Act 2005 (RTI Act). It covers all legislature bodies at the centre, and all administration bodies in the States and in the Union Territories. The Act applies to every single public authority, including those which have been comprised or set up by the Constitution. This implies that Panchayati Raj Institutions, which are in Part IX of the Indian Constitution, are secured by the Act, in this manner giving the peoples an extra apparatus to get to information from these local bodies.""

The Act gives citizens the authority to get to government-held information, including information held at Panchayat level. Citizens can review works, reports, records; take notes, or certified copies of reports or records; take certified pattern of materials; and acquire information in electronic structure from Panchayati Raj Institutions."

Proactive disclosure by Standing Committees of Gram Sabhas

Generally till 31st December of each year annual meeting of the Gram Sabha is to be held. The Panchayati Raj Act 1993 accommodates the setting up of two Standing Committees of the Gram Sabha, i.e., "the Gram Nirman Samiti" and "Gram Vikas Samiti".[16] A Standing Committee is included individuals from Gram Sabha who are Stakeholders of the work allocated to it. The Gram Sabha decides the figure of individuals with the most extreme being twelve.[17] The intention behind having these Standing Committees at the Gram Sabha level is to give an occasion to the village peoples to take part in the progressive activities of their village."

Both Standing Committees have been given the right under to "the Panchayati Raj Act 1993" call for papers, documents and other information and to get ready and submit progress reports of plans and projects falling inside their domain to the Gram Sabha time to time. In doing as such, the Committees empower individuals to take an interest in the administration of their Panchayat. The "Gram Nirman Samiti" has to submit reports to the "Gram Sabha" for sanction with respect to works which is approved for the progress of the village from "Sansad Nidhi" (Member of Parliament Local Area Development Scheme) and "Vidhayak Nidhi" (Individual from Legislative Assembly Local Area Development Scheme).[18]"

Proactive disclosure by Gram Panchayats

The notification of each Gram Panchayat meeting - indicating the date, time, place and agenda should be sent by the Secretary of Panchayat to each office carrier and furthermore set up at the office of the Gram Panchayat seven days before a general gathering and three days before an extraordinary meeting.[19]"

During every Gram Panchayat meeting, a report about the revenue and expense acquired during the period between the last and the current sitting just as the accumulative revenue and expense in the current monetary year up to the current meeting should be put before the Gram Panchayat by the Secretary for discussion.[20] This paper is held at the Gram Panchayat office in the observation of the Secretary and can be gotten to by general society. Moreover, the Secretary should give the returns, description, reports, estimates, statistics or some other information with respect to Panchayat administration.[21]"

Each Gram Panchayat has been enabled to levied charges and fees. In the event that the Gram Panchayat wishes to use this power, nonetheless, it should initially inform the villagers of its motive by making declarations in the Gram Panchayat area and furthermore by setting up a notification in the Gram Panchayat office and at other ordinary spots in the village. Any resident of the village raise an objection to the rate of tax or duty or fee may send his/her complaint or recommendation in writing before the date indicated in the notification. After the conclusion of the rates of tax or fee, the Gram Panchayat should again set up a notification in the office and make a declaration in the village about such changes regarding rates of tax or fee.[22]"

Proactive disclosure by Janpad Panchayats and Zila Panchayats

Once in every quarter the Janpad and Zila Panchayat meetings are held. The Chief Executive Officer[23] sends notice of each sittings in which specified the date, time, place and agenda to each office bearer.[24] The notice ought to in like manner be set up at the Panchayat office seven days before a general meeting and three days before an extraordinary meeting."

In each quarterly Janpad or Zila Panchayat meeting, a report about the compensation and utilization achieved during the period between the last and the current assembling similarly as the all out pay and utilization in the current budgetary year up to the current get-together is put before the people by the Chief Executive Officer for discussion. The public can look at this report or copies can be referenced."

The Janpad Panchayat report should also comprises of information with respected to Gram Panchayats in its jurisdiction. Upto 15 June of every year, the Annual Accounts and Administration Report should be submitted in the meetings of the Janpad and Zila Panchayats. At the same time the report should be released in Hindi and on the notice board of the offices of both the Janpad and Zila Panchayat report were placed.[25]"

ELECTION

Elections give a fundamental vote based space to individuals to choose an individual of their decision who will represent to them and endeavor to satisfy their requirements and interests. Elections at the Panchayat level are a central issue of participation in local governance progress. Information is a fundamental need of individuals if they are to significantly use this most basic of their democratic rights. Better-informed voters mean better-informed choices, more responsive Panchayat individuals and better administration."

73rd constitution amendment Act gives right to state governments to choose the mode of election to the post of leader of the village Panchayat which is Sarpanch. Article 243b(5) of Constitution of India, 73rd amendment, The Madhya Pradesh government decided that Sarpanchs will be elected directly through election. This was viewed as important to make Sarpanch responsible towards individuals. Nonetheless, in spite of this desire, direct election being the greatest resource of the Sarpanch. Neither Gram Sabha nor Village Panchayat members could impact upon Sarpanch as he/she was the direct delegate of the individuals. In the issues of Panchayat, or in the sessions of Panchayat councils, impact of Sarpanch was not subject to the collaboration of other chosen members from the Panchayat which is of panches. This was rather than the proceduregoing on at the Block level and Zila level, where the president is exclusively subject to individuals for his/her survival on the post of president as the election on these posts are done in directly by the individuals. At these levels the election to the post of president have become politicized and definitely contested election by the political parties so much with therefore the legislature needed to ask State Election Commission to hold the election to these indirectly elected posts. The members at these levels know their worth and deal or bargain appropriately. However, at the village level, panches couldn't stack or manipulate the things beside a point and stayed pleased with whatever little courtesy was done to them by the Sarpanch.[26]""

Madhya Pradesh was the 1st state who conducts elections to Panchayati Raj Institutions, in 1994, instantly after the enactment of 73rd Constitutional Amendment Act. Every 5 years Panchayat elections were conducted by the State Election Commission.[27] The Madhya Pradesh State Election Commission is answerable for administration, heading and control of the arrangement of electoral rolls and the arrangement of all elections of the Panchayats."

A scrutiny of state Panchayat guidelines shows that information with respect to Panchayat elections is generally uncovered proactively, particularly related to preparation and display of electoral rolls, release of election program, nominated candidates, election results of the Panchayat."

In Madhya Pradesh for contesting the elections of Panchayat the candidate who take participate in the election they have only a 2 children for such thing Madhya Pradesh government make a policy.[28]"

The Population Policy of Madhya Pradesh states that "persons having more than two children after January 26, 2001 would not be eligible for contesting elections for Panchayats, local bodies, mandis or cooperatives in the state. In case they get elected, and in the meantime they have the third child, they would be disqualified for that post.""

In *Lajja Bai vs State Of M.P. And Ors.*[29], Hon'ble Madhya Pradesh High Court held that "condition to exclude an office bearer of the Panchayat for holding the post: (i) that he should have in excess of two living children, and (ii) out of whom one is born on or after the 26th day of January, 2001."

On 20th September 2016 Madhya Pradesh state assembly passed "Madhya Pradesh Panchayat Raj Avam Gram Swaraj (Sanshodhan) Adhiniyam, 2016" in which stated that under "Swach Bharat Abhiyan" each house should have a toilet, as neatness is a priority of the Gram Sabha.[30]

In such Amendment it is also said that to execute the campaign effectively, it will be compulsory for all the participants of Panchayat elections to have toilets with running water in their house, if such requirement i.e. toilets is not in their house who participates in the election will not be eligible for taking part in the Panchayat elections.[31]"

All those who contest elections to any post under the 3 tier Panchayat system in Madhya Pradesh will also have to give a declaration that they have a toilet at home along with their nomination papers."

Madhya Pradesh Panchayat Raj Act permitted expulsion of Sarpanch from the post if 2/3rd of the total number of Panches from Panchayat and the 3/4th of the Panches present and voting pass the proposal for such impact. Such move can be brought after two and half year from the date on which elected member either Sarpanch or Up - Sarpanch enter their respective office and not during the last 6 months of the Panchayat term expires.[32] This provision was broadly utilized by the panches however it was utilized frequently on the command of opponents of Sarpanch and basically against the women's and dalit Sarpanchs. Also, it was entertaining that, by and large, such eliminated Sarpanchs got re elected by the villagers."

CONCLUSION

As in 73rd Amendment Act of 1992 there is a provision of reservation for women and SC/ST persons for taking part in election and then accordingly seats are also reserved for them but in practically elections were contested by their husbands or family members of women and sturdy or bold person for SC/ST candidate and if they won elections then work also in place of such women and SC/ST person. So, such kind of thing has to be prohibited by the government and has to take strictly action against them who do such type of work. As Madhya Pradesh government make rule that who have more than 2 children's who born after 26th January 2001 has not right to take part in election and who have not toilet in his house has not eligible for taking part in election but actually these rules has not been followed in state because at time of filing a nomination candidates hide this information or give wrong information because as there is not an authority who examine whether candidate gives information in his nomination is right or wrong or whether candidate hide right information about him. So, there should be a authority who examines nomination of candidate or information which candidate provide in nomination because in present scenario even State Election Commission or Returning Officer duty is to examine nomination paper of candidate but there is lacuna in system due to which wrong candidate's nomination is passed by the State Election Commission or Returning Officer.

As after viewing the "Madhya Pradesh Panchayat Raj Adhiniyam, 1993" there is no provision of requirement of education means for contesting election there is no requirement of minimum education of candidate so that illiterate persons also take part in election and then if they win election they not do proper work and fill up their pocket by doing corruption and not doing any work for their constituency. Therefore, Madhya Pradesh Government has to make law or rule for contesting election in which requirement of minimum education has to be mention.

"Panchayati Raj System has brought majority rule government at the grass root level. Regardless of having numerous significant favorable circumstances of this model, it additionally has a few drawbacks."

There are some main loopholes of the Panchayati Raj System which are as follows:-

i. Many of the villagers are uneducated. Same is the situation with the individuals from the village Panchayats. Thus, they are incapable to know the genuine idea of vote based system or democracy.
ii. The village peoples don't have the genuine atmosphere for democracy. The villagers actually have the distinctions in their brains which depend on caste system and envy.
iii. In many villages, the political parties intervene in the working of the village Panchayats. Despite the fact that there is a no place for the political parties in the local self government."

There are some causes due to which many villages not developed

1. The first and significant reason for its moderate advancement is the deficiency of assets. The insufficiency of assets has remained in the fruitful working of the Panchayati Raj. The Panchayati Raj Institutions have been given

almost no assets by the state governments.

2. There is an absence of legitimate participation and coordination between individuals and the authorities like Block Development Officers, District Officers and so forth Authorities neglect to release their obligations all the more effectively and truly.
3. Corruption is likewise a significant reason for moderate advancement of Panchayati Raj working in India. Authorities and the delegates of Panchayats have gotten degenerate.
4. The three-levels don't work as practical specialists. The absence of coordination among the three establishments has hindered its encouraging.

The Panchayati Raj bodies experience a few managerial issues. There is a propensity towards politicization of the nearby organization. Political impedance has been expanding step by step. This has likewise hindered its encouraging."

[1] Dr. Rajinder Singh, *Panchayati Raj System in India: An Analysis*, Vol. I Issue III INTERNATIONAL JOURNAL OF INFORMATION MOVEMENT 63-69, (2016).

[2] HINDU, https://www.thehindu.com/news/national/50-quota-for-women-in-panchayats-planned/article8194551.ece (last visited Sep.20, 2021).

[3] Section 10, Madhya Pradesh Panchayat Raj Avam Gram Swaraj Adhiniyam, 1993.

[4] Department of Public Relations, MP, https://www.mpinfo.org/MPinfoStatic/hindi/factfile/factindex.asp (last visited Sep. 20. 2021).

[5] In the Constitution (73rd Amendment) Act 1992, the term Gram Sabha has been defined as "a body consisting of persons registered in the electoral rolls relating to a village comprised within the area of Panchayat at the village level".

[6] Panchayati Raj Institutions Act PRIA Gram Sabha and Panchayats, New Delhi, 2003.

[7] Rule 6, Madhya Pradesh Scheduled Areas Gram Sabha (Constitution, Procedure of meeting and Conduct of Business) Rules, 1998.

[8] The Secretary of the Gram Panchayat is also the Secretary of the Gram Sabha. The Secretary is under the control of the Gram Sabha and performs the duties that are assigned to him by the Gram Sabha.

[9] Section 6, Madhya Pradesh Panchayat Raj Avam Gram Swaraj Adhiniyam, 1993.

[10] Chapter XIV-A of Madhya Pradesh Panchayat Raj Avam Gram Swaraj Adhiniyam, 1993 on Special provision for Panchayats in the scheduled areas.

[11] Section 2(i), Madhya Pradesh Panchayat Raj Avam Gram Swaraj Adhiniyam, 1993.

[12] Generally a district constituency has a population of 50,000 and is a single member constituency. There are between 10 to 35 constituencies in a district. A block constituency has a population of 5,000 and there are between 10 to 25 constituencies in a block.

[13] Panchayat Act 1962; Panchayat Act 1981; Panchayati Raj Act 1990.

[14] NIRMALA BUCH, STATUS OF PANCHAYATI RAJ IN THE STATES AND UNION TERRITORIES OF INDIA 2000, (Institute of Social Sciences, New Delhi 2000).

[15] Schedule V areas refers to the Fifth Schedule of the Constitution of India which has provisions related to the administration and control of Scheduled Areas and Scheduled Tribes.

[16] Madhya Pradesh Gram Sabha (Procedure of Meeting Of The Committees, Conduct Of Business And Allied Matters) Rules, 2005.

[17] Rule 3(1), Madhya Pradesh Gram Sabha (Procedure Of Committees Meeting Conduct Of Business And Allied Matters) Rules, 2001.

[18] Rule 12(2), Madhya Pradesh Gram Sabha (Procedure Of Meeting Of The Committees, Conduct Of Business And Allied Matters) Rules, 2005.

[19] Rule 3, Madhya Pradesh Panchayat (Procedure of Meeting And Conduct Of Business) Rules, 1994.

[20] Section 44, Madhya Pradesh Panchayat Raj Avam Gram Swaraj Adhiniyam, 1993.

[21] Rule 3, Madhya Pradesh Gram Panchayat (Powers And Functions of the Secretary) Rules, 1999.

[22] Rule 3, Madhya Pradesh Gram Panchayat Obligatory Taxes And Fees (Conditions And Exceptions) Rules, 1996.

[23] The Chief Executive Officer of Zila Panchayat is a Class–I officer belonging to IAS/State Administrative Service. The Chief Executive Officer of Janpad Panchayat is a Class–II Officer.

[24] Section 2(xiii), Madhya Pradesh Panchayat Raj Avam Gram Swaraj Adhiniyam, 1993.

[25] Rule 5, Madhya Pradesh Janapad Panchayat And Zila Panchayat (Annual Accounts And Administration Report) Rules, 1998.

[26] Deepika Gupta, *Reinvigorating Panchayat Raj System in Madhya Pradesh* Vol. 67, No. 1 THE INDIAN JOURNAL OF POLITICAL SCIENCE, 97-108, (2006).

[27] Section 2(xxvii), Madhya Pradesh Panchayat Raj Avam Gram Swaraj Adhiniyam, 1993.

[28] THE INDIAN EXPRESS, https://indianexpress.com/article/india/two-child-policy-in-indian-states-6082879/ (last visited Sep. 15, 2021).

[29] AIR 2008 MP 185.

[30] Rajendra Sharma, *Now, flush-toilet at home must for contesting Panchayat polls*, THE TIMES OF INDIA (Sep. 22, 2021, 9:15 PM), https://timesofindia.indiatimes.com/city/bhopal/Now-flush-toilets-at-home-must-for-contesting-panchayat-polls/articleshow/55515587.cms.

[31] Rahul Noronha, *Toilets a must to hold Panchayat offices in MP*, INDIA TODAY (Sep. 26, 2021, 1:30 PM), https://www.indiatoday.in/india/story/toilets-a-must-to-hold-panchayat-offices-in-mp-327480-2016-07-05.

[32] Section 21, Madhya Pradesh Panchayat Raj Avam Gram Swaraj Adhiniyam, 1993.

Printed by Libri Plureos GmbH in Hamburg,
Germany

9 798886 298352